Ethnomethodology: How People Make Sense

Warren Handel

Southern Illinois University

Ethnomethodology: How People Make Sense

Prentice-Hall, Inc., Englewood Cliffs, New Jersey 07632

Library of Congress Cataloging in Publication Data

Handel, Warren H.
    Ethnomethodology, how people make sense.

    Bibliography: p. 159.
    Includes index.
    1. Ethnomethodology.   I. Title.
HM24.H365   301.01'8   81-5178
ISBN 0-13-291708-4 (pbk.)   AACR2

Editorial/production supervision
        by Virginia Livsey
Cover design by Miriam Recio
Manufacturing buyer: Edmund W. Leone

Printed in the United States of America

10   9   8   7   6   5   4   3   2   1

Prentice-Hall International, Inc., *London*
Prentice-Hall of Australia Pty. Limited, *Sydney*
Prentice-Hall of Canada, Ltd., *Toronto*
Prentice-Hall of India Private Limited, *New Delhi*
Prentice-Hall of Japan, Inc., *Tokyo*
Prentice-Hall of Southeast Asia Pte. Ltd., *Singapore*
Whitehall Books Limited, *Wellington, New Zealand*

A COMMON SENSE PROOF WITH PRACTICAL ADVICE
AND A COMMENT ON THE GENRE

THE PROOF

He has enough who is content. *Italian Proverb*

And. . .

Who is content is rich enough. *German Proverb*

But. . .

Definition of *enough:* "All there is in the world if you like it."
Ambrose Bierce

And. . .

"You never know what is enough until you know what is more than enough." *William Blake*

And. . .

"None know the unfortunate and the fortunate do not know themselves." *Richard Saunders*

So. . .

No one is content with his own lot. *Portuguese Proverb*

Therefore. . .

"Advise the mature 'be satisfied with what you have,' but tell the opposite to eager youth." *Edward Alsworth Ross*

Because. . .

"Evidently organisms adapt well enough to 'satisfice'; they do not, in general, 'optimize.' " *Herbert Simon*

And. . .

To pursue happiness is to flee contentment. *Yiddish Proverb*

And. . .

"If a man is not content in the state he is in, he will not be content in the state he would be in." *Erskine Mason*

But. . .

"One who is contented with what he has done will never become famous for what he will do." *C.N. Bovee*

And. . .

Nothing ventured nothing gained. *American Proverb*

THE PRACTICAL ADVICE

"Think of three things, Whence you come, Where you are going, and to Whom you must account." *Richard Saunders*

THE COMMENT

"You get more credit for thinking if you restate formulae or cite cases that fall in easily under formulae, but all the fun is outside saying things that suggest formulae that don't formulate—that almost but don't quite formulate. I should like to be so subtle at this game as to seem to the casual person altogether obvious. The casual person would assume that I meant nothing or else I came near enough meaning something he was familiar with to mean it for all practical purposes. Well, well, well." *Robert Frost*

Contents

Chapter 3

AN ILLUSTRATED PROGRAM: PRACTICAL REASONING OR THE COMMONSENSE ATTITUDE   53

Chapter 4

FURTHER SPECIFICATION OF THE COMMON SENSE ATTITUDE: CROSS PURPOSES IN NATURAL SETTINGS   79

Chapter 5

PRACTICAL REASONING IN MEASUREMENT AND CATEGORIZING 103

Chapter 6

CONVERSATION ANALYSIS   129

Chapter 7

THE STANDPOINT OF THIS STUDY   149

Preface

This book is a secondary source, written with the needs of a student audience in mind. As does any secondary source, this one condenses and organizes an evaluative selection of the information available. To some extent, the selection and organization of information are impelled by the intellectual content of the primary sources and by the sentiments of the intellectual community. Still, there is considerable discretion. Exercising it responsibly is, at the same time, the most important privilege and most burdensome challenge of writing secondary presentations. As Dave Macon, the social critic and star of the Grand Ol' Opry, put it, "The only thing that we can do is to do the best we can." I'm fond of this book and satisfied with it for the most part. I hope you like it too.

Secondary presentations for students pose special problems of expression. Primary academic sources are not exoteric, nor are they meant to be. They are extremely elliptical and employ many vocabulary and stylistic conventions that make them cryptic to all but a trained, specialized audience. Students are no more members of this specialized audience than is the general public, but they are apprenticed to it. As do other nonacademic audiences, students require that the information be presented without oversimplification and without using the specialized shorthand in a confusing way. In addition, students must be taught the specialized shorthand so that they can become full members of the academic community. Unlike popularized presentations, then, books for students ought to include the specialized technical vocabulary. This one does.

I have adopted several policies in my efforts to include the academic shorthand in a lucid way. I present the empirical content of the studies that I discuss in nontechnical English. These straightforward descriptions of events that stand apart from the theoretical discussions are essential, in my opinion. One cannot understand *how* people make sense until one can see *that* they make sense. The theoretical implications of the studies must sometimes be stated in technical terms. I define the technical terms and explain their significance before using them. Some technical terms that are widely used in the primary studies proved unnecessary for this presentation. I define some of them and indicate how they are used, even when they are not employed otherwise in this book. Familiarity with those terms is necessary in reading the primary studies. My criterion for deciding which terms to define and treat as technical was simple. Whenever I had doubts that a student would understand a word, I looked it up in an unabridged dictionary (usually the *Random House Dictionary of the English Language*). If the dictionary definition did not match the academic use of the term, I considered the term technical. My goal was to make this book self-contained—to make it independent of having particular prior training—except for the use of a good, preferably unabridged, dictionary.

The relative shortness of this book constitutes an additional constraint on its contents. I chose to emphasize empirical studies and to include discussions of theory and philosophy only when they were necessary to comprehend the mainstream of ethnomethodological work. The historical development of ethnomethodology, and many of its intellectual antecedents, have been underrepresented relative to the composition of the primary literature. I have not contrasted ethnomethodology to other schools of thought; neither have I systematically differentiated and contrasted the several variations on the ethnomethodological theme. These are omissions by design. I consider them to be the topics most expendable in an introductory presentation. It is my impression that students are generally uninterested in the details of academic disputes. They seem to be more concerned with questions admitting of demonstrable answers. Of course I may be projecting. As usual, it is not what you don't know that causes trouble; it is what you know that ain't so.

Several people deserve credit for their contributions to this project. Edward Stanford, the sociology editor at Prentice-Hall, conceived the project and helped to define several of the parameters within which it was constructed. Norman Denzin, Barry Schwartz, Marshall Sumsky, and Don Zimmerman read and commented on a nearly final draft of the manuscript. They made several excellent suggestions, many of which I followed. Victoria Fricke, Donna Stephens, and Gay Michael served as my graduate assistants at various stages of this project and were very helpful in completing many important tasks. Judith Handel has read and commented on portions of this project beginning with the letters I sent to Prentice-Hall even before there was a formal proposal. She often serves as the final arbiter of whether major revisions are warranted.

Warren Handel

Ethnomethodology:
How People
Make Sense

1

What Ethnomethodologists Study and Where They Stand While They Study It

INTRODUCTIONS

Normally, texts in sociology put their most abstract foot forward. At the heart of the discipline (and of each of its specialties) is a group of empirical studies and theoretical interpretations of the facts or observations in them. This material is generally referred to as the "literature." Usually, though, before authors get around to reviewing the literature, they devote a chapter or two to outlining the most fundamental and abstract characteristics of the discipline. These include the defining of topics of study within the discipline, the common questions that underlie and inspire the diverse studies, and the characteristic ways in which these questions are asked and answered. Even more abstractly, it is common to consider the nature of the entire scientific enterprise and to assess sociology's standing within it. Oddly, these ventures into the history and philosophy of science are more common in the introductory texts, whose readers are generally unsophisticated, than they are in specialized texts.

There is a method to this introductory madness. By raising a series of questions first, the diverse studies and theories can be presented as a coherent, if partial, set of answers. Otherwise, the studies might initially appear to be miscellaneous, and the discipline might initially appear to be a catalog of unrelated facts. This initial impression is important. The writer of sociology texts is an ally of the instructor in attracting and holding the student's attention. Among romantic authors, the spoken motive is to draw initial interest to a discipline that is not only fascinating once one becomes involved but also important to informed collective social action. The realists among us acknowledge intellectual commitment and the potential for increased enrollment among our spoken motives. In a cynical frame of mind, we are apt to speak firmly (and romantically) about our own intellectual commitments while characterizing students strictly in terms of their administrative appeal. (Enrollment, credit hour production, and cost are frequent concerns. This way of characterizing students, incidentally, is reminiscent of the body count approach to news about our Vietnamese adventure a few years ago.) The issue of royalties from textbook sales may arise.

Whatever the spoken motives, it is important not to lose the attention of students before they have had adequate exposure to the discipline. If students become impatient with the lack of organization before they read enough studies for the connections among them to become apparent, they withdraw from the course. Some might actually withdraw bureaucratically. But requirements being what they are, and dealing with registrars being what it is, they'd most likely coast through as comfortably as possible and not return for additional courses. Even in a quarter or semester, even in a five-week crash summer school course that lets everyone have some kind of summer vacation, a concluding chapter that suggests how the field is organized might be too late.

There is, too, some madness in this method. Without knowledge of the studies, the questions and the interests of sociology may be very difficult to understand. They are likely to appear artificial, pompous, or sterile. They may appear to belabor the obvious. The writer who begins with these abstract considerations provides organization from the very start. In fact, such a writer provides organization before there is any content to organize. This avoids the peril that the reader will find the discipline incoherent. Alas, but as usual, there is a price. The reader must take an extremely abstract, sparsely illustrated set of organizing principles seriously until enough content has been presented to justify it. Expecting a course in sociology, whatever preconceptions that involves, a student should be excused for wondering why he or she is reading about the history of Western thought, the scientific method, and the major subdivisions of a field about which he or she doesn't yet know. The resolution of this wonderment provides a second set of reasons to lose interest.

Practically speaking, good introductions are padding between a rock and a hard place. There is a practical problem: How to attract attention quickly and hold it until the student has a chance to make his or her judgments. The problem is compounded by the variety of pressures and interests that bring students to introductory classes in the first place. A student fulfilling a requirement for his or her major is a different beastie from one choosing a general education course because it is offered at the right time of the day. Both are different from a student who is interested in sociology as a sidelight to his or her main interests or because he or she thinks that it is part of a well-rounded education. The standardization of introductions indicates tacit agreement on the best way in which to approach students.

I have not been describing introductions as a way of enlisting your sympathy for my dilemma. At least, I have not been doing it entirely for that reason. This chapter promises in its title to tell you what ethnomethodologists study and where they stand while the study it. I have already begun to do that. Ethnomethodologists study the activities in which people engage while they are attempting to make sense. I have discussed introductions from an ethnomethodological point of view. An introduction is the product of practical reasoning that begins with a need to make sense of sociology for a student who cannot be assumed to know anything about it. A variety of practical motives compels writers to write introductions as they do and compels instructors to select the books that they do. To solve their practical problems, instructors and writers must presume background information about their students—level of sophistication, of basic skills, of motivation, and so on. This information supports predictions about how students will act. Plans and reasoning are predicated on this information. So is the style of writing. The background information is voluble, though. Any instructor or writer worth his or her salt can change from seeing students as interested and alert to seeing them as poorly prepared if a course does not work out well. This is more comforting than changing one's self-conception.

The question of where one stands to do ethnomethodology is partly metaphorical. Concretely, a class looks very different to an instructor than to a student, if only because they are facing in opposite directions. If they faced in the same direction, things would look more similar to them. The literal sense of having a standpoint is to have a physical location and to have one's perceptions influenced by obstacles and aids to perception. In addition, the idea of a standpoint includes any background knowledge, routines of conduct, and practical motivations that a person brings to a situation and that influence thought and action. The Jew and the anti-Semite cannot resolve their differences by physically facing in the same direction. They might not even be willing to do that if one had to stand behind the other. Finally, thought and action are influenced by the behavioral routines of others.

Social scientists are no less human than their subjects and no less subject to the laws governing human conduct. Ethnomethodological studies explore the influence of peoples' standpoints (or perspectives) on their thought and action in great detail. To explain why people act as they do, ethnomethodologists examine their physical and social circumstances, their habits and the habits of those around them, their background knowledge, and their practical motives. These factors influence how people make sense of their environment and respond to it. The standpoints of ethnomethodological studies are as important as the standpoints of other attempts to make sense of events. I shall be paying considerable attention to them. If you skipped the preface, you have already missed some information about how this book was assembled. There is more in Chapter 7.

In the reminder of this chapter I shall review three ethnomethodological studies in detail. I shall indicate the range of things counted as sense-making activities in these studies and the standpoint of each. Chapter 2 will be soon enough to begin addressing the technical conclusions that are drawn from these studies and others. If I am going to lose your interest part way through this little book, I believe you'll be happier knowing about Agnes, the practical methodologist, than about ethnomethodologists' interests in the philosophy of science.

AGNES, THE PRACTICAL METHODOLOGIST[1]

Agnes is the pseudonym of a nineteen-year-old person who was identified as a male at birth and was raised as a boy until high school. At puberty Agnes's normal male genitals were accompanied by female secondary sex characteristics.

---

[1]   This discussion is based on Garfinkel (1967), ch. 5).

Agnes grew large, rounded breasts, female-shaped hips, soft skin, and a typically female distribution of body hair. During her senior year in high school she left home, moved to another city, changed clothes, had her hair styled, and attempted to begin a life as an adult woman. At age eighteen, she applied to the UCLA medical center for a sex-change operation. Her measurements at that time, for the statistically minded, were 38-25-38. Specifically, she wanted to be castrated and to have a vagina surgically constructed. Although she could not, of course, bear children, such an operation would permit normal sexual relations as a female and be undetectable in routine gynecological examinations.

Garfinkel gathered information about Agnes while participating in an investigation of her eligibility for surgery. Before surgery, Agnes was thoroughly investigated to be sure that she was morally and psychologically, if not physically, a woman. Garfinkel's information originated, for the most part, in a series of interviews that he conducted with Agnes during the investigation. It is useful to differentiate between two types of information available through his interviews. The first type is Agnes's version of events that were known by Garfinkel only through her descriptions. To live as a woman prior to her operation, Agnes had to conceal her physical anomalies from others. In the course of the interviews, Agnes described many of the techniques she employed to conceal her physical irregularities and to overcome her inexperience as a woman. After all, a nineteen-year-old is expected to have more than three years of experience in the ways of her gender. The methods she developed for being accepted as a woman in the community prompted Garfinkel to refer to her as a "practical methodologist." She lacked theoretical knowledge of how society worked. Still, she developed methods or techniques for manipulating the meaning of social situations on a practical basis. We might also refer to these methods as activities used to make sense of herself as a woman.

The second type was information about Agnes's conduct during the investigation. Garfinkel directly observed this conduct. To be judged eligible for the operation, Agnes needed to convince the hospital staff that she was morally and psychologically a woman. During the interviews she was observed to manipulate the information she presented to bolster that case. She idealized her past by emphasizing her female characteristics and her successes as a woman. She minimized any favorable male experiences and failures as a woman. She freely admitted to troubles that could be solved by the operation.

It is important to draw this distinction between the two types of information. Garfinkel's accuracy in reporting her methods for passing in the community was contingent on the accuracy of his understanding of her conduct during the interviews. To put it crassly, she may have lied successfully about her activities in the community and their success as a means to prove her eligibility for the surgery. She may have been an even better practical methodologist than Garfinkel suspected.

Before plunging into the details of the techniques Agnes employed to live as a female and to convince the UCLA staff that she had done so, the peculiar notion of a "woman with a penis" wants consideration. When pressed, we are inclined to define gender in a biological way, usually in terms of the nature of the genitals. During the Olympic games we are reminded that more sophisticated biological tests may be required to establish who is really a female. However, in our daily lives we are able to differentiate between males and females without direct observation of their genitals and without miscroscopic examination of their chromosomal structure. We use other criteria to make this differentiation: clothing, visible aspects of appearance, voice, sex-typed behavior.

These criteria are less fundamental than are the biological ones. But, more often than not, the biological details are irrelevant to our relationships as well as unexamined. This is not merely a matter of tentative judgment, cautiously made while awaiting the real biological evidence. In most of our relationships, the reality of the genitalia is never relevant, and direct evidence is never observed. Even in those cases in which genitals are observed, for example, in locker rooms, we have already assigned one another to a gender and have made social commitments based on that assignment.

Even in a world of modest clothing and sex-typed behaviors, our biological characteristics remain fundamental to our sexual identities. Agnes could not have simply presented herself to others as a woman with a penis and could not have treated the penis as a casual conversation piece. Although they are not important as evidence, the genitals are vital to our sexual identities as an empirical and moral assumption. Our genitals are expected to be appropriate to our gender. Incongruities are not just factually remarkable. They are also morally unacceptable. Men should have penises. Women should have vaginas. Even less striking irregularities have moral implications. A man should not be impotent; a woman should be able to bear children.

In a way, the genitals that are relevant to most of our social relationships are not the physical or biological ones. The relevant genitals are social. They are assumed and morally expected to be in place, to be biologically normal, to be functioning properly, to be the sort of equipment a man or woman in our culture ought to have. Genitals are not present as evidence used to differentiate between the sexes. They are there as a matter of definition, and people are credited with having one kind or another as a result of being identified as a man or woman.

Agnes possessed a social set of female genitals but a male set of biological ones. For her, the distinction between the two was both threat and salvation in her social relationships. The threat was obvious. At any time that her physical genitals were observed, she would be reclassified. She would no longer be a woman but, given her other physical characteristics, not a transvestite either. She would be a freak, an outcast from the gender-typed world. The salvation is that the assumption of biological normalcy is deeply held and assumed without doubt.

Genitals are small enough and infrequently enough revealed to leave Agnes with a manageable, if difficult, task, the task of living as a female without revealing the disqualifying physical evidence. Her social genitals, possessed by virtue of profoundly held cultural expectations, made that task easier by discouraging any interpretation of her behavior as a sign of her not being a real woman. On the other hand, the moral character of the social genitals made it imperative to succeed by establishing severe degradation as the penalty for failure.

Agnes is certainly a curious and interesting person. Her case has an importance, though, that has little to do with her specific concealment problems. Agnes's general problem was to present an image of herself or preserve a given reputation. To understand how her situation applies to you, stop for a moment and think about the difference between "social kindness to one's family" and "actual kindness to one's family," between "social honesty" and "actual honesty." Remember that, after every grotesque crime, after every especially brutal case of child abuse, after every embezzlement by a pillar of the community, after every personal misfortune titillating enough to attract the press, every day, in short, some neighbor, friend, or member of the family appears on television shaking his or her head sadly and saying, "He or she seemed like such a nice man or woman." In fact, for any characteristic you know to be true of anyone, perform this exercise: Think of that truth as a "social truth" or reputation and try to remember how you came to know that fact, how that reputation was earned. Ask yourself, "How do I know that?", and keep asking. As soon as this exercise becomes uncomfortably disorienting, move on. You've got the point.

Passing in the Interview

Garfinkel refers to the activities by which Agnes achieved and maintained her status (image, reputation) as a female, "passing." Her interviews with Garfinkel and with staff psychiatrists were part of the testing that preceded her sex-change surgery. The purpose of the investigation was to determine the merits of the surgery she requested. In addition to the physical risks of extensive surgery, the staff was concerned about her social and psychological adjustment after the surgery. To satisfy themselves, they tested Agnes's personality and probed her motives. All the time, they were attempting to estimate her ability to adjust and to assure themselves that she was psychologically a woman and not, for instance, a homosexual.

From Agnes's perspective, the problem was to convince the staff that she was a normal woman suffering from a physical deformity. She attempted to portray the penis as no more than that—a physical defect like a scar or a birthmark. As a woman she would naturally be relieved to have the deformity removed. As a woman, surgery would end her problems of adjustment, not begin them. Thus, in the interviews, Agnes spared no efforts to appear the normal, natural female. She minimized her past as a male, downplaying most of her life. She minimized the importance of her penis, admitting it to be no more than a physical deformity. She dissociated herself from homosexuals and other sexual oddities, refusing even to discuss possible difficulties with others who had undergone similar surgery. The penis was her only trouble. Surgery was the obvious solution.

This sense of her situation was presented through a variety of activities. When questioned about childhood, she denied having ever fit in as a boy. Even as a child, she said, even before her secondary sexual characteristics developed at puberty, she was always a female, mistakenly treated. She denied having childhood friends, claiming that she could never act as she was meant to act with either males or females because they all related to her as a male. As her figure developed she disguised it with loose clothes and avoided company to remain inconspicuous. She gave no details about gym classes in school. She admitted to no sexual pleasure from her male genitals and no sexual feelings for women. Sexually, the penis was inert.

Agnes also concealed aspects of her present situation and recent past. She would not allow her boyfriend, mother, or female roommate to be interviewed. This made it impossible to corroborate or refute her version of events. She exaggerated her successes as a woman and refused to acknowledge negative aspects of her situation. She evaded questions. She tried to guess what the interviewers wanted to hear before answering. She lied.

Passing in the Community

The description of Agnes's efforts to pass as a woman in the community are based on the information given to the medical staff under the conditions just discussed. Many of the specific activities that Agnes employed to establish herself as a woman were obvious. She wore women's clothes and makeup, she wore her hair in a feminine style. She checked the place for females on forms and used women's restrooms and locker rooms. The secretarial jobs she took were traditionally female. But there were more interesting activities that were more intricate as well. These required Agnes to surrender considerable spontaneity for their success. People with matched biological and social genitals can sustain their gender identity with no special preparations. A variety of situations though, those that involved the risk of physical exposure, required Agnes to be furtive and wary to sustain her identity as a woman.

To get a job, Agnes had to undergo a physical examination. Her plan was to allow the doctor to examine her only above the waist. If a more thorough examination was demanded, she planned to refuse, claiming modesty. If necessary, she would leave, forfeiting the job but saving her identity. As it happened, the doctor did not insist on a pelvic examination, but another complication arose. A urine sample was needed. Instead of an enclosed toilet with a door, the office was equipped with a urinal. A nurse might enter the room and see Agnes while she was exposed. Agnes claimed to be unable to urinate rather than risk exposure and promised to return later with a urine specimen. For fear that urinalysis might reveal her unusual sexuality, Agnes borrowed a urine sample from her roommate. She explained that she had an infection that might cost her the job.

Sustaining relationships with friends and her female roommate presented some problems. At home she and her roommate maintained privacy and avoided nudity. Agnes insisted on her privacy. Dating posed problems. Agnes avoided pickups. She didn't drink, fearing that she might lose control. She favored multiple dates and house and church parties over solitude with a male. She didn't kiss on first dates, she avoided necking and, by all means, petting below the waist. Going to the beach required both planning and wary flexibility. Agnes wore tight, constricting underpants and a bathing suit with a skirt. She changed from street to swimming clothes only in a closed bathroom or bedroom, never in a public bathhouse or a car. If privacy was not available, she sat on the beach in her street clothes and said she didn't feel like swimming.

Two of Agnes's concerns were less episodic and less easily handled. First was maintaining her relationship with her boyfriend. The continuing relationship with her boyfriend led to increasing pressure for sexual intimacy. At the same time, the continuing relationship undermined her reasons for refusing. Agnes told the hospital staff that, ultimately, she explained her physical condition to her boyfriend. She refused to explain how she convinced him of the facts, however, and she never described their sexual activities. The boyfriend was not interviewed. Thus, there was no confirmation that he actually understood the nature of the physical anomaly. Agnes's vagueness about this relationship was a chronic problem in her attempts to convince the staff that she was a normal woman. If her undetailed accounts could be believed, managing her boyfriend's sexual demands was a chronic problem.

Agnes's second chronic problem was her lack of experience as a woman. One continuing difficulty was her lack of suitable biography. Whenever tales of the past were being exchanged, Agnes could not contribute without threatening her current identity. She could lie, of course, but she would have to make up many complex lies and keep them straight. Agnes was also not trained for her activities as a woman in the slow, usual manner. She dealt with this lack of experience by approaching situations as a "secret apprentice." While learning to cook favorite family dishes from her boyfriend's mother, she was also learning to cook. She listened to judgmental gossip carefully as instructions for correct conduct. When discussing styles and sewing, she used the occasion to learn standards of modesty, craftsmanship, and so on. This is, she was especially attentive to the views of others and adopted them readily to compensate for the lack of views of her own.

Thinking About Passing

Thus far we have not considered the reasoning processes that must support and organize the kinds of activities that Agnes performed. Taken one at a time, her passing activities challenge our sensibilities more than our imaginations. But considered in concert, considered as an ongoing way of life, those activities are quite dramatic. More important, they reveal some aspects of the attitude with which Agnes approached social situations. If Agnes has seemed alien to you thus far, her attitude should make her seem less so. It is your attitude, too, and mine.

First, we must consider Agnes's ability to plan her activities to minimize the threat of being discredited. Agnes assumed that certain expressive activities have routine and predictable consequences for how one will be perceived. For example, if a person checks the place for "female" on a job application, he or she can assume that he or she will be defined as a female unless some contrary evidence arises. All of Agnes's manipulative attempts to be defined as a woman were based on the premise that, to a practically satisfactory extent, she could anticipate the meaning of her activities and appearances to others. Her version of the particular implications of particular activities and appearances allowed her to anticipate what must be avoided and what must be done.

Second, Agnes recognized that ongoing events are sufficiently fluid and unpredictable to frequently require plans to be adjusted or abandoned in the course of acting them out. For example, Agnes's plan to limit the physical examination required for her job was sound enough. Still, it did not anticipate the detail that there would be no enclosed toilet for collecting the urine sample. Similarly, Agnes could plan a day of swimming and sunbathing, but she must be prepared to modify her plans if she could not dress in private. She could never be sure of this until the last minute, until she was at the beach. And so, at the last minute, she must have frequently needed to change her plans and explain her decision to remain in street clothing as best she could. She could plan not to engage in petting below the waist. But she must respond to advances as they occurred—and in a manner appropriate to the circumstances, as must we all.

Third, Agnes was aware that our experience of the world is vulnerable to manipulation by extraordinary tactics. Secrets can be kept; lies can be told; the truth can be stretched and bent. Agnes was more aware of this, perhaps, than most of us because she was so thoroughly engaged in actively approaching situations manipulatively. Since sex typing is so pervasive, her particular secret required pervasive efforts. The unpredictability of happenstance, the surprises that are shot through routine events, set limits on our vulnerability to manipulation. In Agnes's situation, control of her secret depended, finally, upon control of her clothing and of being touched. An automobile accident that led to her being undressed involuntarily could, at any time, expose her secret. So could something as undramatic as her roommate's barging into her room without knocking.

Finally, Agnes assumed that the ability and desire to manipulate appearances was commonplace. As she was aware of others' vulnerability to her efforts, she was aware of her vulnerability to theirs. She assumed that they were like her, although their secrets may have been different. This was clearest in her relationships with the hospital staff during her presurgery investigation. She doubted that they were forthright in their motives. She feared that, despite what they said, they might decide to amputate her breasts and make her a physically congruous male instead of female. She feared that the questions were traps. Hence her evasions, lies, and exaggerations.

The Standpoint of the Study

Garfinkel's study of Agnes was conducted steadfastly from Agnes's point of view, as Garfinkel saw it. Her reports were the basis of his description of her passing activities in the community. Her success in shielding her family and boyfriend from the interviewing process precluded corroboration of her methods of concealment and of the degree of success she reported. In effect, Agnes's passing in the community can be understood as passing in the interviews. Whatever else she accomplished, Agnes passed in her interviews as a woman with a penis who had succeeded in living as a woman in the community.

The importance of choosing a standpoint can be indicated by considering the cause of Agnes's physical anomaly. Originally, Agnes told the doctors that she had always felt like a girl and that her development of female secondary sex characteristics was confirmation of her real nature. Her penis was just a cosmic joke. This story was compatible with the medical tests, was accepted with some reservations by the medical staff, and was an important consideration in deciding to perform the sex-change operation.

After the operation was performed, however, Agnes changed her story. At the onset of puberty, she had taken hormones prescribed for her mother. These hormones were a better explanation of the physical facts than was the previous story. Suggestively, after confessing her adventure with the hormones, Agnes allowed her mother to be interviewed. The results of that interview are not reported.

We must consider Agnes's stories about her life as a woman with this known subterfuge in mind. Her physical anomaly was real, whatever the cause. Agnes may have lived as a woman by sustaining extreme modesty in the ways outlined. But one of the interns met her boyfriend and thought he was a homosexual. We could, with little trouble, construct another story about Agnes. In this story, her peculiar anatomy equips her relationships with her roommate, boyfriend, and dates quite differently.

The issue at stake is not finding an ideal standpoint, one that would get at the truth of the matter. Rather, we must be aware that adopting various standpoints leads to adopting various truths. Garfinkel's decision to adhere to Agnes's standpoint, as he saw it, makes Agnes's intentional manipulation of social circumstances to foster a desired impression clear. It also allows a clear view of the attitudes that support such manipulation.

But leaving other standpoints out of account obscures other information. While Agnes was busily manipulating social situations, what were her companions doing? What impression did Agnes actually foster? What were the routines and limitations of her companions' perceptual activities that made their experiences vulnerable to manipulation? What were they taking for granted? What surprises did they overlook? Did people notice details that seemed to suggest that something odd was afoot and chose to ignore their implications? Or did they actually restrict their intake of information and reduce the amount of such information available to them?

A concrete example may clarify the possibilities. Bats navigate by sonar. They emit signals and receive echoes in sufficient detail to hunt flying insects in the dark. Bat caves remain unchanged for thousands, perhaps millions, of years except, of course, for the depth of guano. Although there are obstacles to fly around, those obstacles are fixed. Bats flying in and out of their caves do not fully utilize their sonar. To save energy, they fly blind, by memory. This has been strikingly demonstrated by placing obstacles in bat caves that an attentive bat could easily avoid. The bats fly right into them (Griffin 1976).

People are not bats. Our social world is not a bat cave. And people with secrets are not experimentally manipulated obstacles in an otherwise static environment. But the metaphor is not unduly far fetched. To conserve the resources involved in observing and considering events carefully, and to avoid being distracted from more important matters, people observe their world in a routine, habitual manner. Their attention to routine matters is reduced. These routines and habits, the manner in which people attend to events, is crucial to understanding the pheonomenon of passing. Indeed, it is crucial to understanding communication of all kinds.

Two standpoints are involved in communication: the standpoint of the sender of information and the standpoint of the receiver of information. Both are involved in making sense. A standpoint is not a person. It is a set of circumstances. Each person takes both standpoints simultaneously in the process of interacting with others. Agnes, for example, had to observe others to adjust herself to contingencies that arose unexpectedly. Seeing the urinal as a threat to her secret indicated her attention to the situation in terms of her practical needs. While not noticing her penis, to what were the others with whom she dealt attentive?

There is a third standpoint that bears consideration. That was the standpoint of Garfinkel and the rest of the hospital staff. They were involved in both receiving and sending information. But their practical interests were distinct from those of Agnes and those of the others in the community. Attention to their standpoint would have made available still different truths about Agnes's situation. Which of her activities helped to convince the hospital staff to proceed with the surgery and which caused them to doubt that the surgery was appropriate? Put another way, which of Agnes's techniques were successful, and which not? More important, perhaps, by taking the standpoints of Agnes as a sender of information and her companions in the community as receivers of information simultaneously into account, a view could be provided of how a social reality is constructed of the truths held by the various participants. How do people with different understandings of what is true manage to get anything done?

A final standpoint needs to be considered. Yours. What are you to make of the morass that was Agnes's situation? Perhaps I can help you out here. Do not worry too much about what Agnes really is finally, once and for all. Really, Agnes is different things to different people, different things at different times. What she is for anyone at any given time depends on what information has been received about her and the standpoint at which it was received. The observer's own practical motives, habits of perception, and desires to sustain particular impressions of himself or herself are as fundamental to what Agnes is to the observer, as are Agnes's own characteristics.[2] If your practical motives include understanding ethnomethodology, save the details of Agnes's case to entertain your friends. As a fledging ethnomethodologist, the important thing to notice is how much work everyone has to do to sustain the sense of social situations.

I will be discussing the work in technical terms later. For now, remember that to be a woman Agnes had to manipulate others in many ways and then convince the medical staff of her intentions. To understand Agnes, the medical staff conducted scientific tests, interviewed her, and so on. The dramatic character of the case makes the work more easily visible. However, probably without conscious effort, we all do things that convince others of our gender and decide about the genders of others.

---

[2] For structural, sociological constructions of how a person's identity might vary from audience to audience see Erving Goffman (1959); and Robert Merton (1957).

There is another reason to avoid spending time and effort attempting to determine whether Agnes is a male or female: it cannot be done. First, Agnes is intriguing exactly because the facts of her case do not allow her to be confidently assigned to either gender category. As the two terms are defined, she is neither fully male nor fully female, but a bit of both. Our binary gender categories, which we use with unquestioned confidence in most cases, is simply inadequate to the facts of Agnes's case. She was apparently able to live part of her life as a male and part as a female. The peculiarity of her situation draws our attention to what is involved in establishing gender. Second, as we have seen, in Agnes's case differential access to information results in diverse judgments of what Agnes is. You might pore over all the facts at your disposal and decide to your own satisfaction what Agnes is. But that will not make the various opinions of others go away. You would simply be adding one more appraisal to the already confusing list. Agnes is such a dandy example of how identities are categorized because she defies careful categorization completely when some sets of facts are known but appears quite ordinary when other sets of facts are known. The diversity of opinions about Agnes is not a result of careless or incompetent judgment by some and it cannot be corrected. Rather, the available categories—male and female—do not allow Agnes to be placed confidently in either category when the facts we know are known.

THE POLICE ON SKID ROW[3]

Peace Keeping

Peace keeping is the problem-solving portion of police work that does not typically involve arrest. As a result, formal records are not regularly produced, and there is no close supervision by the courts. In peace keeping, the officer employs commonsense expertise and detailed knowledge of the area that he or she patrols to keep order—to solve domestic and interpersonal problems. Among the peace keeping tasks common to skid row are controlling the level of such illegal activities as gambling and vice, keeping skid row inhabitants geographically confined, settling family disputes, controlling crowds, and protecting drunks, vagabonds and other incompetents, and criminals from themselves and each other. On skid row, the police act as conscience and social arbiter for the members of the community.

Although it accounts for a large proportion of police time and resources, peace keeping is not considered to call for professionally skilled police work. No special training is provided, and novice police are expected to keep the peace immediately without initial guidance. Although standardization was not

---

[3]   This discussion is based on Bittner (1967a).

imposed by training or supervision by the courts, the police were in remarkable agreement about the nature of skid row as a patrol situation, and skid row policemen developed highly standardized peace keeping techniques. They were not aware of this consensus, however, until Bittner informed the individual police of the ideas of the others. This information was shared when Bittner sought to check the accuracy of his understanding of the police point of view by explaining it to the police he had studied. Their surprise was testimony to the habitual, unexamined, unattentive manner in which the routines of perception operate. Particular problems, as they arise, are attended closely and carefully, utilizing unattended assumptions and habits as resources in making particular decisions. Knowledge of peace keeping activities, then, ought to provide insight into some of the unanswered questions in the study of Agnes. Agnes's ability to manipulate social situations depended on the routinization of perceptual scrutiny. The study of peace keeping activities reveals much about that routinization.

Structural Demands of Police Work on Skid Row

To the police, peace keeping on skid row amounts to responding to the general structural demands of police work in the special environment of skid row. The police are charged with the supervision of licensed premises including taverns, barber shops, shoeshine stands, and stores. Many businesses are exploited as the site of illegal activities such as gambling. Police assume that these activities cannot be stopped, but they value cooperation from the proprietors in controlling the level and publicity of the activities. Cooperation is measured by involving the license holders in a complex exchange of favors. Illegal activities, known to the police, are continued. The license holders provide information to the police and convey messages and pressure from them to the community. The license holders become a network of informants. In addition, they must remain acquiescent to casual inspection of their premises (without warrants) and be generally responsive to requests for favors.

The ability of the police to impose this arrangement is bolstered by an important resource provided by their official position. The right of the police to decide to arrest a person or to issue a citation implies their discretion to not arrest that person, even if a violation has been committed. Thus, not arresting someone, not issuing a citation or otherwise condoning violations, can be granted as a favor by the police. The withdrawal of this favor is a substantial pressure for a compliance with police requests.

The police are routinely called upon to settle domestic disputes and other quarrels. The network of informants is a vital source of information about routine domestic arrangements. This information provides the background for understanding occasional crises. A husband's complaint that he has been locked out of his home by his wife, for example, would demand less attention if it was well known that this happened regularly. In dealing with quarrels, the threat of arrest and the favor of letting someone off help calm situations.

The police bear a special responsibility to protect people who are less than completely competent. Some people are actually designated as less than competent by law. Among these are the mentally ill and children. Others are not officially entitled to special attention but are known, in fact, to have a knack for getting into trouble. Among these are drunks, vagabonds, and known criminals. Skid row is inhabited almost entirely by various marginally competent types. Hence the ubiquity of peack keeping as opposed to, say, crime solving on skid row.

Skid Row Personalities and Police Tactics

To the police, skid row inhabitants are a collection of individual tragedies and souls in need of saving. Collectively, the inhabitants can be controlled and the skid row life-style geographically confined. The typical skid row inhabitants are regarded as lacking the competence or inclination to live normal lives elsewhere in society. They approach each other, and expect to be approached, on that basis. Planning and commitment are virtually absent. The inhabitants live for the moment with no sense of practical or moral necessity to schedule events. Shopkeepers and a few transients that are temporarily between jobs are possible exceptions to this typification of the skid row personality. But they are not fully trusted either.

In understanding and controlling situations that arise on skid row, the police gear their activities to a high frequency of fortuitous accidents. They do not expect people to maintain a schedule and, therefore, to be easily located. Nor do they expect implied or spoken commitments to be fulfilled in good faith. Although they may be honestly offered, commitments succumb routinely to unexpected events. Skid row personalities are weak and easily tempted from the path of the moment. Intentional exploitation is common, too. This moment-to-moment life-style reduces the impersonal control of sustained commitments and increases the need for active police control.

In practice, the police keep abreast of up-to-date gossip about who is working, and where, current relationships, and whatever habits are regular enough to help locate a person. For example, knowing that a particular drunk frequents a particular bar, especially when a certain hooker is there off duty, helps the policeman find that drunk if he wants to. The rarity of such regular habits, though, imposes a style on peace keeping operations. Since it is so hard to find people and since relationships and other circumstances change so frequently, the police cannot pursue one matter at a time to its conclusion. That procedure would result in their spending most of their time looking for people who are hard to find and who might no longer have the problem by the time they were located. Instead, the police keep track of many simultaneous projects that all need to be taken care of. In their rounds, they are alert for information about all of them. They deal with each problem as the opportunity arises. Thus, although their own rounds are regular, the order in which their work is done, except for handling crises, is quite fortuitous.

This understanding of skid row life has other important implications for police tactics. The reduced competence of skid row inhabitants encourages the police to take active control of their lives, to intrude by demanding information and using their authority to dictate behavior for the person's own good, and to make moral judgments for them. The police demand the right to casually enter and inspect premises and order people around, even in the absence of legal offense. Since most inhabitants of skid row are almost always technically guilty of minor legal offenses, the police assert their right to take these considerable liberties with the threat of arrest. Thus, a person who doesn't allow a policeman to see what is causing the bulge in his pocket may find himself arrested for public drunkenness. At least that possibility will be mentioned in trying to convince him to account for the bulge. Finally, the lack of continuity and commitment and the erratic scheduling of skid row life encourages the police to feel that arresting people causes them no great hardship. In a problem situation, then, the police feel free to arrest the person whose removal from the scene will most completely remedy the problem. This may not be the offender in the legal sense. Also, the police feel relatively free to arrest people for nonlegal reasons, even where they are doing nothing out of the ordinary.

A detailed account of a specific case may help clarify how this peace keeping strategy appears in action. The police are often called upon to settle disputes or to defuse situations that appear to have a potential for imminent violence. In such situations, the skid row police do not worry about legal or moral blame. Instead, they do what must be done, arrest who must be arrested, to best resolve the problem. Since arrest is not viewed as a severe inconvenience, the practicalities of keeping order take precedence over legal niceties. In one such situation, a man was known to have received a sum of money. He was expected to get vulnerably drunk and, with vaguely homosexual intentions, seek out a male companion. His likely companion was a rough type, by reputation, who could be expected to beat him up and take the remaining money. Arresting the companion would not help. Another companion would be found of more or less the same type. So the potential victim was arrested for his own protection before he became helplessly drunk. The arrest was intended to get him a good meal, sober him up before the money could be stolen, and prevent violence. On the other hand, the arrest occurred before any crime and resulted in the incarceration of the potential victim. The understanding that order must be kept on skid row without relying on the decency of the citizenry justifies this solution to the problem.

This characterization of skid row life is the view of the skid row police, as Bittner sees it. This standpoint differs from the standpoint taken in Garfinkel's study of Agnes in two very important ways. Garfinkel conducted his study from Agnes's point of view; Bittner conducted his from the point of view of the skid row policeman. Agnes is a single person. Garfinkel's study analyzed social situations as they were seen by one person, as he understood Agnes's view. The skid row policeman is not a single person; rather, it is a social role. Bittner's study represents his construction of how various persons, thrust into a similar social situation, typically understand and respond to it. Each is a case study, but of very different kinds of cases. These are two different ways of approaching the study of how sense is made. Sense is made by individual people; sense is made by types of persons.

The second difference in standpoint involves the distinction between sending and receiving information. Agnes's chief concern was to make sense of situations by fostering a particular impression of herself. Her activities were primarily intended to control the flow of information. She wanted to influence the definitions and interpretations that others arrived at and, through them, their conduct. The skid row policeman, though, is portrayed as primarily interpreting information. His understanding of the structural demands upon him as a policeman; his understanding of the nature of skid row life and the personalities of skid row inhabitants; and his understanding of the important factors in interpreting and responding to situations are all part of his routines of perception. So are the attention to problem solving and the style of using the law to achieve practical ends. The study of Agnes shows that fostering a particular impression can be strenuous work; the study of the skid row policeman shows that keeping track of what is going on can be strenuous work. As a matter of fact, these are complementary aspects of the same work.

The police on skid row are not only seekers of and responders to information, Fortunately, Bittner's study includes a discussion of the policeman's concern to foster the impression of his authority and control of his district. Police tactics on skid row require that they be allowed to casually inspect and enter premises, ask personal questions, insist upon getting up-to-date gossip, and establish themselves as to the conscience of the community by making and imposing moral judgments. In part, these rights are secured by coercion, especially by the threat of arrest. But, for the most part, compliance is smooth. Members of the community grant the policeman authority in these matters and do not often need to be persuaded of their power.

The policemen are very concerned with maintaining the appearance of that authority at all times. They are alert to challenges to their authority and bring their resources to bear to maintain it whenever challenges arise. For example, the policemen allow themselves to be addressed in familiar and vulgar terms. They also allow their orders to be the subject of rude verbal responses and even partially ignored. But these privileges are restricted to situations in which no challenge to authority is implied. The presence of an audience to witness the rude response may lead to arrest for a remark that would be laughed off and forgotten if it were made on any empty street. Even a show of disobedience such as getting off the street slowly and with a show of indifference may be allowed. However, the presence of observers to this manner of obeying an order transforms the situation into a test of will and authority and may lead to arrest.

To the policemen, their unquestioned authority is essential to the smooth operation of their tactics. To lose authority is to lose control over the network of informants, to lose rights of access, to lose the right to give any but technically legal orders. It is an unacceptable degradation of their station. In sustaining the show of authority, the police remain alert to situations that present challenges to that interpretation of their stature and make preserving that appearance their first priority. That is, they act like Agnes.

THE SOCIAL ORGANIZATION
OF JUVENILE JUSTICE[4]

Assessing Character in an Organizational Setting

Cicourel's study deals with juveniles who have become involved, unfortuitously, with the police. Often, these juveniles have had previous encounters with disciplinary authorities. They have typically had both disciplinary and academic trouble in school. Often, too, they have a history of prior contacts with the police, courts, probation authorities, psychological testers, and other agents to whom we delegate problem youths. In each instance, the interest of the authorities may be attracted by either a dramatic incident, such as a theft, or a chronic problem, such as repeated truancy from school. In either case, the history of official interest and action in the youth's case is compiled in a file which is consulted and enlarged in each new contact.

Among the critical considerations as to what will be done to the youth is his or her character as it is assessed by the responsible agency. Character is the term commonly used by juvenile authorities for the complex of judgments that sum up the moral worth and prospects of the juvenile in trouble. Although character judgments are especially consequential in this official context, the term has the same meaning as in ordinary usage. Does the juvenile need counseling? Is the juvenile intellectually capable of adequate performance in normal school curricula? If so, why is he or she failing? Can the juvenile be counted upon, if returned to the community, to stop doing the things that have caused trouble in the past? The answers to these questions, and others, constitute the

---

[4] This discussion is based on Cicourel (1968).

character of the juvenile. Even seemingly factual questions, such as those regarding IQ and reading ability, take on a moral tone because they are implicated in the decision of how to treat the juvenile and what to enter into his or her record.

The making of a character judgment, then, is an instance of sense-making activity. The juvenile and his or her family is called in to account by the authorities. The stakes are high. If the authorities make a negative character judgment, the juvenile may be expelled from school, required to undergo treatment, or sent to a juvenile detention center. Each agency involved consults the juvenile's file for official accounts of previous transgressions; the juvenile and his or her family offer their own versions of events. Our attention will be focused on a few aspects of sense making that are more clearly exhibited than in the other studies we have considered.

The coherence of character judgments.   We are, all of us, chronically unrealistic in our expectations about the results of sense-making activities. We expect, after working to make sense, to have made sense. We expect to have produced a reasonable, comprehensible, coherent account of events. We are not chronically confused and disoriented. We make enough sense of things to get by. But, on the other hand, close scrutiny reveals that our sense of things is vulnerable to artifice and protected by habits of inattention. Cicourel's study of bureaucratic character judgments makes this point especially well.

Two senses in which character judgments are incoherent stand out. First, the character of the individual, the sense that is made of him or her as a person, is judged differently by various others and at various times. Second, the several character judgments made of individuals involved together in some event may not allow a coherent account of the event. For example, in describing and re-describing the event, now one, now another person may be judged blameworthy; now one, now another person may be victim. For illustration, I shall describe the disposition of three cases in the same agency. The juveniles were involved in, among other things, a single incident. The incident, and the juveniles involved in it, appear differently in versions developed at different times and in the contexts of separate cases.

A thirteen-year-old girl was expected to meet her date at a dance. Instead, she left with some other boys who took her to a secluded place and provided her with liquor. She got drunk and had intercourse with at least one of the boys. She stayed with the boys for two days, even after becoming sober. They provided her with clothes to replace her soiled ones. Finally, they dropped her off near her home.

The boys depicted the girl as a slut who had willingly been involved in intercourse with one of them and had wanted to have intercourse with more of them. They characterized the boy who admittedly had sex with her as the victim of this more experienced female. The police, however, initially characterized her as a sweet girl who was victimized and assaulted by older boys. While the case was still being processed, however, the girl was apprehended at a party that disbanded upon the arrival of the police. The girl was extremely drunk and admitted to having engaged in intercourse with ten boys, give or take, each of whom had told her his name was Robert. Robert, of course, was involved in the first incident. The girl said she loved him. At this point, official speculation was that the first incident had given her a reputation. She had quickly become known as someone who, if drunk and confused, would have sex with anyone who called himself Robert. However, as the investigation proceeded, it became clear that she had a previously unrecorded history of getting drunk and engaging in sex. The official judgment was that she did this to hold onto boys or assure their friendship. Ultimately, the girl was defined as sufficiently disturbed to require institutionalization in a state mental hospital.

In the disposition of her own case, Linda, our thirteen-year-old, was increasingly held to be the cause of her own troubles. Her parents were increasingly faulted as well. She did not bear any criminal responsibility, but the series of incidents were finally attributed to flaws in her character. Clearly, the initial sense of her as a victim of trickery and/or assault eroded as the case proceeded.

But, at the same time, Denis, one of the boys involved in the original incident, was also being processed by the same juvenile agencies. In addition to the sexual escapade, Denis had a history of petty theft, arson, and other offenses. In handling his case, the juvenile authorities characterized the sexual incident as an assault and an instance of taking advantage of a possibly innocent girl. Denis was described as encouraging Linda to get drunk and as having attempted intercourse with her. Both facts were denied in the testimony, but they remained in the official version of the incident as it appeared in his file. While Linda was being defined as disturbed and sexually promiscuous in her own case, she was being defined as the victim of the boys in another. Moreover, in these two versions, the responsibility for the incident was differently assigned.

I am not suggesting that one of the parties must be blameless. However, there is something discontinuous about a story which, as told in two files, describes the drunkenness and promiscuity of a girl in a single incident as, alternately, the victimization of a young innocent girl and an episode in her already established, and continuing, pattern of similar activities. There is a sense in which both are reasonable descriptions of what happened. But there is also a considerable shift in responsibility for the incident and for the way the characters of those involved are defined.

Cooperation in sense-making.[5]   Establishing one's character is not necessarily a solitary activity. Agnes's case is striking, in part, because her peculiar secret made it imperative that no one be fully informed. As a result, she could not fully enlist the support of others in her efforts to establish an identity. Juvenile court cases are quite different in that respect. The activities of the

[5]   See Erving Goffman's discussions of teamwork and dramaturgical loyalty (1959).

juveniles' parents, for example, are very important to the way in which the juvenile is judged. In effect, coming from a good home can be a character assessment of the child, even though it appears to depict his parents.

Linda's father, for example, appeared to the juvenile authorities to be as sick as Linda. This judgment of him was developed as a result of his conduct during the investigation of his daughter. It was very important in the decision that she needed treatment outside the home. Denis's parents expressed indifference to the seriousness of his activities, including the sexual episode and incidents of theft. They dismissed them as normal, youthful behavior and discounted his culpability and their own. In addition, they resisted the officials' threats that Denis might be incarcerated. Ultimately, despite those threats, he was left at home.

The case of Robert, who was also involved in the incident was even more striking in this regard. He was regarded as incorrigible in school and as having a psychopathic or prepsychotic personality. His mother suffered periods of severe depression. A probation officer recommended that Robert be placed in a state hospital or special school. Later, a probation officer and referee recommended that he be treated as a criminal and committed to the youth authority. However, his family provided a lawyer who was able to reconstrue all the troubles as psychological, rather than as criminal, ones. Robert remained at home. The provision of a lawyer was another sort of sense-making effort by his parents and further expanded the sense in which one presents one's character cooperatively with others.

The judgment of character may be cooperative as well as its presentation. Bittner's study dealt with a special kind of official judgment: those made by single officers based on personal knowledge of a neighborhood and on firsthand observations. Although a network of informants was involved, the informants were not particularly trusted and there was no indication that their words were taken at face value. In these juvenile court cases, though, character judgments may be collective decisions, upon which various parties must agree. In addition, knowledge about the person to be judged may come from many sources, often compiled in the file. The juvenile files contain entries from schools, previous contacts with the police, doctors' reports, probation officers' reports, and so on. In addition, those actively involved in a case may share information that never appears in the file. Each person who examines the file must interpret and rely upon the observations of others, incorporating them into his or her own evaluation of the case. In this way, they all work together, even while apart.

By consulting the file, the perceptual and presentational routines of all contributors are indirectly involved in any current evaluation. To fully understand a police action, we must know, for example, how the schools evaluated the juvenile and how school files are assembled and disseminated. The two institutions are interlocked in compiling official judgments of the juvenile. In our modern world of dossiers and the exchange of information among institutions, a full account of a juvenile court decision is likely to require investigation of the perceptual and presentational routines of many other institutions. Unless we decide to truncate our investigation, unless we decide that enough is enough, we might find the entire social structure implicated in a full account of a single episode. That is a grand vision, but it does impose an impractical task upon researchers.

The Standpoint of the Study

Cicourel wrote his study from the standpoint of the researcher. He recognized that his own routines of perception and his own involvement in the incidents are important parts of the sense he is able to make of them. He describes them along with the activities of the authorities, juveniles, and their families. The effect is striking and disorienting.

By this device, an addition is made to the description of the activities of those involved in processing the juvenile, as Cicourel saw them. We are also treated to some insight into how Cicourel saw them, as he saw that. For example, Cicourel's original intent was to follow several cases through every stage of official processing. But that became impossible due to outside commitments and to the simultaneous occurrence of hearings in the several cases. As a result, all stages in the processing of all cases could not be observed. For another example, Cicourel recorded many of the conversations on which he reported. But, often, technical difficulties or noise resulted in only a partial recording. Thus, literal transcriptions of conversations are interspersed with summaries of what was said based on his notes and memory. These adjustments to inconvenience were part of how he saw events as he did.

Descriptions of data-gathering techniques are standard in research reports. But Cicourel added an additional dimension to that practice by including them as part of the substance of the report rather than as a relatively separate matter. He did not treat his observations as an artifact of his technique in a perjorative sense. Rather, he acknowledged that his operations as a maker of sense stood unavoidably between his subjects and his readers. The sense of events that it provided to his readers was a result of his efforts as well as of the efforts of his subjects. If he wrote a novel or fabricated his report, the sense would be provided entirely through his efforts.

By differentiating the standpoint of the researcher from that of the presenter or interpreter of information, I do not mean to imply that the researcher does something other than observe and interpret. Rather, I mean to emphazie that the practical motives of the researcher are distinct from those of the subjects. In addition, the researcher's routine—for example, having job obligations that require leaving the places where the subjects fulfill their job obligations—constrain the researcher's ability to observe the subjects and give him or her a distinctive perspective on events.

SUMMARY

Making sense of things requires considerable effort. There is thinking to be done. Plans must be laid; plans must be revised; events must be attended and disattended; information must be interpreted. This thinking may be done by several persons on a cooperative, if not completely coherent, basis.

There is information to be conveyed to others. This involves a wide variety of overt conduct: hiring lawyers, borrowing urine samples, telling drunk thirteen-year-old girls that your name is Robert, arresting people for their own good, and so on. There is no end to it. Anything we do will, among other things perhaps, help make sense. Notice, please, that sense is being discussed as a product that is actively made and continuously remade. This is in accord with ordinary usage such as, "Here's my exam. I hope you can make sense of it." But there are some parts of ordinary talk and activity that go unnoticed.

If we are going to avoid some truly horrendous sentences later, when some theoretical sense is made of making sense, we are going to have to agree upon a term that covers all these diverse activities, mental and overt. Otherwise we will be stuck with far worse phrases than "sense-making activities," which is bad enough. Many synonyms have already been used. Forms of "interpretation," of "definition," of "construction," among others, have already been interspersed with forms of "making sense."

The term *accounting* (and its forms) will be used to refer to all these activities; the term *accounts* to refer to content; the term *accountable* to refer to moral imposition and adequacy. This family of words is one of the several used in the ethnomethodological literature. Its advantage over the others is simply this: The technical use of the terms coincides fully with ordinary usage. I recommend that you look up "accounts," "accountable," and "accounting" in *The Random House Dictionary of the English Language; Webster's New International Dictionary,* second edition, unabridged; and/or the *Oxford English Dictionary.* Read all the definitions and illustrative uses. I believe that you will find that the various sense-making activities that I have described are all accurately called accounting. I believe that you will find some additional suggestions. Looking things up in a good dictionary is, in general, a fine way to gather accounts, helpful in giving a good account of oneself, and, if asked, not a bad way to account for one's time. Besides, you may be held accountable for the knowledge.

A FORMAL EXERCISE

This is the first of a series of related exercises. If all goes well, in a few weeks you will be prepared to do your own field observations and prepare a straightforward, original ethnomethodological report. The first exercise is to practice describing commonplace events so that others can clearly understand them.

Gather in comfortably sized groups. If you have friends in the class, do not stay in the same group with them if that is possible. Each person in the group will describe, in turn, what he or she did before class. After each description, the rest of the group should ask questions until the sequence of events is clear to them. Be picky. (Your instructor may want to raise the pickiness level by joining in.) When the questions become too picky, go on to the next description. This will be somewhat unpleasant, I expect. Stick it out. If you attend closely to the questions that are raised, your ability to include the facts that the hearer needs will improve.

2

The Philosophical
Concerns
of Ethnomethodology

Accounts, then, exhibit some interesting characteristics. When examined closely, the reasoning employed in accounts is not strictly logical, and the information contained in them is not precise, final, or consistent. Still, reasoning is done; communication is accomplished; activities are coordinated. How?

It is axiomatic to ethnomethodology that everyday accounts are not mistaken, careless, or sloppy approximations of traditional logical argument. But it is also axiomatic to ethnomethodology that everyday accounts are not strictly logical. Accounts differ from traditional logical argument, but not by error or imprecision. Accounts differ from traditional logical argument by having a different formal structure.

Two bits of jargon crept into the last paragraph—the terms *traditional logic* and *formal structure*. In apology, I offer this account of them. The term logic refers to several different, highly formalized systems of rules for correct argument and inference. In addition it refers to the sense of particular arguments and situations. Traditional logic is just one of those sets of formalized rules. Among philosophers, traditional logic is understood to refer to rules associated with Aristotle, although modified by his successors. Traditional logic is the subject of elementary logic courses. Among sociologists, however, the term logic, without qualification, almost always refers to traditional logic. Hence the term formal structure, which is synonymous with logic as defined in the dictionaries and as used by philosophers, but not as it is used by sociologists. The term formal structure, then, is an attempt to avoid confusion between logic and traditional logic.[1]

Is it reasonable to doubt that traditional logic is an adequate approximation of everyday reasoning? One of the main emphases of this chapter, and the central philosophical concern of ethnomethodology, is to demonstrate formally that it is. My strategy will be to consider two questions and to show that each, treated carefully, leads to difficulties for traditional logic. These difficulties are peculiarities of meaning, similar to those exhibited in the accounts described in Chapter 1. Strict application of traditional logic, then, cannot eliminate those difficulties. They may appear to be carelessness or error, but they can not be avoided by greater care. They are, rather, problems that arise because traditional logic is not an appropriate model of everyday accounts. They will remain forever mysterious unless their occurrence is explained in terms of a different formal structure.

We are about to play a word game. It has been aptly called "square-the-circle-till-you're-tired." In this game, words are taken seriously. They are used as precisely and consistently as possible. Then the words are manipulated logically. The objective is to apply the rules of logic accurately until we are led to un-

[1] Further elaboration of the varieties of logic and the specific characteristics of traditional logic are found in the *Encyclopedia of Philosophy* (Edwards 1967).

acceptable conclusions and then to discover why the unacceptable conclusions occur. The discovery of simple mistakes in logic or definition is no fun. The fun begins when we must profoundly alter our understanding of reasoning or of using words to explain the unacceptable results of logical thinking and how we avoid them in everyday life.

Traditional logic and this game have one rule that you will need to keep in mind: the *law of the excluded middle*. Every category or term must be well defined to be manipulated logically. When a category is well defined, everything is either in the category or it is not in the category. Nothing is both in the category and not in the category; nothing is neither in the category nor out of it. There is no "middle"; no ambiguous borderline case. Consider the category "horse." To use the term in traditional logical argument, the term must be defined so that everything is clearly either a horse or not a horse. If this rule seems too innocent to cause any trouble, reflect on the category "woman."

TWO QUESTIONS

How Tall Is Still Short?

This question is a member of a family of questions whose roots can be traced back more than two thousand years to the Greek philosophers called Sophists.[2] The issue involved is sometimes called "the heap" and sometimes "the bald man." These dignified names for the problem derive from two of the earliest questions used to pose it: "How many grains are there in a heap?" and "How many hairs can be removed from a hairy man's head before he becomes bald?"

Let us begin by agreeing, for the sake of argument, that any adult person who is 4 feet tall is short. Let us consider, then, the person who is 4.0001 feet tall. Is that person also short? Well, then, what about the person who is 4.0002 feet tall? 4.0003 feet tall?

The drift of this argument should be clear by now. We continue to increase the height under consideration by increments of .0001 feet. It will take some time, but eventually we will be considering people 6 feet tall and 10 feet tall for that matter. Sooner or later, a choice must be faced. We could continue to call everyone short. If that becomes uncomfortable, we could begin, at some point, to call people not short. But, so long as we follow the procedure I outlined, to make that shift requires us to say that a person at some height is short, but another who is taller by an amount imperceptible to the unaided eye, say, .0001 feet, is not short. If we refuse to name a precise boundary for the concept short, to define the concept well we will soon be calling people 7 feet tall short. In fact, we will soon be calling every person short. To make matters worse, if

---

[2]   This discussion follows the argument of the Max Black (1970a).

we begin at 10 feet, an assuredly tall height and subtract tiny amounts, we will soon be calling everyone tall as well. This is our unacceptable result. We must pick a precise point and claim, absurdly, that an imperceptible increase from that point marks the transition from short to not short or we are driven to the absurdity that everyone is short (and also tall).

Why don't we just draw a boundary on shortness, then, and have done with it? All that is required is to pick a height to which any addition, no matter how small, is sufficient to change a person from short to not short. The difficulty is that selecting a height in that way is not appropriate to the meaning of the term short. The boundary would be placed differently by different people and even by the same person at different times. (Select a height, if you'd like, and compare it with the ones your neighbors select.) Whether a person is short or not depends, in part, on the practical or theoretical interests at stake. A short basketball player is a tall jockey. The term short, as it is used colloquially, is not precisely defined. It is, in Black's term, a loose concept, a category in which some things do not clearly and finally either belong or not belong. Further, Black argues, this looseness is not accidental but, rather, is intended among users of the term. No sensible person would consider it possible to specify the precise height at which shortness stops. There is no specific, well-defined boundary between short and not short, and to impose one would indicate a misunderstanding of the term.

Now, at least, we know why the attempt to play logically with the term short led to absurd conclusions. Short is a loose term, and traditional logic only applies to well-defined concepts. But this is not a solution; this is the problem itself. How frequent are loose concepts? If there are many of them, then traditional logic is inapplicable to a large variety of situations. Well, there are a lot of them. In fact, all empirical concepts are loose in the same way as shortness. This is most obvious in terms that make quantitative comparisons or judgments— short, bald, fat, rich, cheap, intelligent, and so on. But it is also true, as we have seen, with respect to the term "woman," with respect to assigning responsibility, and with respect to deciding who has violated the law and what law has been violated. The effect of conceding that shortness is a loose concept, then, is to disqualify the application of traditional logic to empirical matters. That is why the problem has intrigued philosophers for so long. And since there is no defensible precise and final boundary for shortness, we cannot resolve the difficulty by defining the term and insisting that common usage is in error.

Some philosophers are prepared to admit that logic is inapplicable to the empirical world. Logic, and with it philosophy, are restricted to the realm of well-defined concepts. This concession has two drawbacks. First, it makes philosophical reasoning inapplicable to real events and situations. For example, systems of ethics are developed that define "the good" precisely but only in ideal terms that do not properly apply to any ethical decisions involving factual considerations. Second, this approach leaves philosophy with nothing to say about the conduct of reasoning with empirical concepts in everyday use and in science.

Black suggests a different resolution to the dilemma. He is committed to the applicability of traditional logic to empirical matters. His resolution, then, is to describe how reasoning is done with loose concepts and to defend the validity of that reasoning within appropriate bounds. Black argues that loose concepts are not always troublesome. There are cases in which the terms can be applied unquestionably. A person 4 feet tall is short. In these cases, logical manipulation of the concepts will not cause trouble. We will run into no logical difficulties because we call a person who is 4 feet tall short or a person who is 6 feet tall not short. But somewhere between these heights we will indeed encounter difficulties. We will be uncertain as to whether a person is short or not short. People will disagree. We will change our minds. Attempts to draw inferences about the person based on the judgment that he or she is short will prove unreliable. People will sometimes wear short sizes and sometimes not; people will sometimes be able to spike a volley ball and sometimes not. Predictions will be erroneous; deduction will lead to false conclusions. Logic will not apply.[3]

In creating this zone, Black attempts to reconcile the looseness of empirical categories with the law of the excluded middle. He suggests that loose concepts are sometimes not precisely and finally applicable in empirical cases. That is what makes them loose. On the other hand, sometimes these categories can be confidently and finally applied. In those cases, one can reason with them as if they were well defined. Some things are clearly short or not short. About them, you may reason logically. Some things are not clearly short or not short. About them you must reason warily because the application of traditional logic may lead to untoward results. Overall, the concept is loose, but in clear cases it may be manipulated as if it were well defined. The clearness of the empirical instance substitutes for clear definition of the term.

The nature of the vague cases must be considered. The boundaries of these problematic areas cannot be precisely fixed. We cannot place a single boundary between short and not short. For the same reasons, we cannot place two boundaries that precisely distinguish the ambiguous cases from the clear ones. So this borderline category is as loose as any other empirical category. But it is not worthless on that account. Black argues that the looseness of empirical concepts is a matter of consistency and confidence in judgment. A height is not, in itself, short or not short or borderline. Rather, in some cases we are confident and reliable in our judgments, in others we are not. The borderline category is not a group of cases whose definition is unclear; it is a group of judgments about which we are uncertain and inconsistent even though we are able to make provisional judgments. These provisional judgments, however, because they are apt

---

[3] In the same way, the terms "man" and "woman" can usually be used unambiguously despite the existence of troublesome, ambiguous cases such as Agnes's.

to be reversed, do not support logical manipulation. Thus, as our confidence in judgment decreases, it becomes necessary to place correspondingly little confidence in any inferences we draw. In the extreme, logic becomes, in effect, completely inapplicable.

Black's solution acknowledges an element of skill and activity in reasoning beyond the application of rules of logic. There can be no precisely and finally fixed rules for applying empirical terms. Still, one must apply them. One must decide when the terms have become too imprecise for the practical or theoretical occasion. This is a skilled estimate, not completely formulated. One must then apply logic with as much confidence as the case allows and constantly check the results of reasoning against empirical events to be certain that one has not misplaced that confidence. Weighing the adequacy of the results of reasoning is another loose judgment. The results must be judged against the standard "good enough for now."

Black's analysis of reasoning with loose concepts, then, recognizes the relevance of practical, imprecise judgment in the reasoning process. It is an important step toward an ethnomethodological approach because it seriously considers how people actually reason. Ethnomethodological studies, though, attempt more thoroughly to replace traditional logic as a model of the formal structure of everyday reasoning. We can see more clearly how this effort is justified by considering some questions implied by Black's analysis, but left unanswered. First, Black's analysis implies that judgments are made without precise rules for guidance. One must decide that a case fits a particular loose category and with a particular degree of confidence; one must check the results of reasoning to be sure they are reasonable. How are these judgments made? There is a borderline region of doubtful judgments. Logic does not apply to these cases. How do people reason when they are unsure? Are we reduced to trial and error? To blind intuition? To confusion and anomie? Is there a formal structure to activities and reason undertaken in doubt?

Black's analysis implies that either there are (1) two or more distinctive reasoning processes used in empirical matters, each employed with its appropriate level of confidence in one's categorizations, or (2) a realm in which logic does not apply and there is no formal structure to reasoning and action. Ethnomethodologists are convinced that practical reasoning and action have a formal structure and also that this unspecified formal structure, when fully elaborated, will encompass all reasoning with loose concepts. That is, it will replace traditional logic.[4]

---

[4] This fundamental change in the way in which reasoning is formulated is one of the bases for calling ethnomethodology fundamentally different from the rest of sociology. Wilson (1970) clearly shows the sociological implications of different understandings of how practical reasoning is done.

Would You Like to Hear of a Race Course That Most
People Fancy They Can Get to the End of in Two or Three
Steps, While It Really Consists of an Infinite Number of
Distances, Each One Longer Than the Last?[5]

The race course in the question is a syllogism, the most fundamental form of argument in traditional logic. Carroll's proof utilizes an axiom of geometry, Euclid's first proposition. This axiom contains no necessary loose terms, and the proof applies to any syllogism whatever, even when it is expressed in well-defined mathematical terms. Thus, the difficulties that arise in argumentation are not the result of loose terms. Instead, Carroll shows that some difficulties of argumentation are inherent in traditional logic itself.

Carroll's proof begins with a standard syllogism:

(A)   Things that are equal to the same thing are equal to each other.
(B)   The two sides of this triangle are things that are equal to the same thing.
(Z)   The two sides of this triangle are equal to each other.

The tortoise is willing to accept (A) and (B) as true statements but is not willing to accept (Z) without further proof. The tortoise challenges Achilles to explain why it must accept (Z), to compel the conclusion that (Z) is true. Look carefully at (A), (B), and (Z). (Z) cannot be false if (A) and (B) are true. And so Achilles answers, if (A) and (B) are true, (Z) must be true. It follows logically. The tortoise accepts the argument of Achilles on the condition that it must be added explicitly to the proof.

(A)   Things that are equal to the same thing are equal to each other.
(B)   The two sides of this triangle are things that are equal to the same thing.
(C)   If (A) and (B) are true, (Z) must be true.
(Z)   The two sides of this triangle are equal to each other.

Certainly if the tortoise accepts (C) as true, it must accept (Z) as well. But the tortoise is nothing if not methodical. Before accepting (Z), it wants Achilles to explain why it ought to do so. Why must (Z) be true if (A), (B), and (C) are true? Achilles examines the three statements to which the tortoise agrees and observes that they compel one to accept (Z) as well. And so he answers the tortoise. It follows logically. If (A), (B), and (C) are true, (Z) must be true. The tortoise is willing to accept this argument as true, but only on the condition that it be made explicit and added to the other steps.

---

[5]   This question was posed by the tortoise to Achilles in a logical proof cast as a fable by Lewis Carroll.

(A)   Things that are equal to the same thing are equal to each other.
(B)   The two sides of this triangle are things that are equal to the same things.
(C)   If (A) and (B) are true, (Z) must be true.
(D)   If (A), (B), and (C) are true, (Z) must be true.
(Z)   The two sides of the triangle are equal to each other.

The infinite number of steps between (A), (B), and (Z) is apparent. So is the sense in which each is longer than the last. The tortoise has treated the statement, "It follows logically," differently from Achilles. For Achilles, that statement is an indication that something is obvious and that no further argument is needed. For the tortoise, it is just another argument. The issue between them is the acceptance of fundamental assumptions about what is obvious without further proof or elaboration.[6]

For our purposes, the tortoise taught Achilles that logic is not a neutral, universally acceptable set of rules. It rests on the acceptance of axioms and definitions. If those axioms and definitions are not accepted, or if they are replaced with others, a different formal structure is generated. Specific questions, pursued diligently, raise difficulties for the application of logic to everyday reasoning. One possibility, raised by this consideration of logic as a method of reasoning, is that the difficulties arise because the axioms of everyday reasoning are different from those of traditional logic. So ethnomethodologists argue.

REFLEXIVITY AND INDEXICALITY: TWO ETHNOMETHODOLOGICAL COMMITMENTS

Ethnomethodologists have made two commitments concerning the formal structure of accounts. Together, they summarize the difficulties inherent in trying to apply traditional logic to everyday reasoning, formulate fundamental characteristics of everyday reasoning, and provide a research program. The two commitments are

1.   All accounts are *reflexive*.
2.   All accounts are *indexical*.

At least the first of these is axiomatic. The status of the second commitment is not clear. The indexicality of accounts may be an implication of assuming their reflexivity axiomatically, or it may be axiomatic itself. You can judge for yourself as the two are discussed. It is an important commitment, in either case, and will be discussed here as a separate topic.

[6]   For additional discussions of this proof, see Winch (1958) and Black (1970b). Those who are fond of mathematical puzzles should note that Carroll has applied Zeno's paradox to steps in an argument rather than steps in space.

Reflexivity

Originally, the term *reflexive* was used in grammar and logic. In logic, a reflexive relationship is one that something could have with itself. For example, everything is equal to itself; equality is a reflexive relationship. Nothing is greater than itself; "greater than" cannot be a reflexive relationship. In grammar, the term is used in a related way. A reflexive verb is one whose subject and object are the same. "Shave" is a reflexive verb in "I shave myself." In the same sentence, "myself" is a reflexive pronoun. In a sense, the reflexive verb describes a relationship of an actor with itself. The action is taken upon the agent of the action. The barber may shave me or himself. When he shaves me, the verb is not reflexive; when he shaves himself, it is. By extension, the actions themselves are often called reflexive when the person acts upon himself. Shaving oneself is a reflexive action. So are feeding oneself, pampering oneself, deluding oneself, and improving oneself. The term reflexive has been extended to include the action upon oneself or relationship with oneself as well as the grammatical form we use to describe them.

Ethnomethodologists argue that all accounts are reflexive. All accounts are not in the distinctive grammatical form called reflexive; they are not even all linguistic. Rather, using the extended sense, ethnomethodologists argue that all accounts have a reflexive relationship with themselves and take some action upon themselves, regardless of their content and regardless of the medium in which the account is expressed and regardless of their grammatical structure, if any. We can begin to understand the nature of the reflexivity of accounts by examining the special case in which the content of accounts is concerned. Theories and empirical descriptions of perception, language, nonverbal communication, reasoning, or any other aspect of accounting are accounts about accounts. Since they are accounts, whatever they say about accounts will apply to themselves as well. That is, they are reflexive. An example of this type of reflexive relationship has been built into this book. The first few pages serve as an introduction to ethnomethodology and are also about introductions. That introduction, then, describes itself. It is reflexive.

Ethnomethodologists are very concerned with this aspect of reflexivity because they are convinced that all empirical accounts are loose. When this scientific assessment is applied reflexively, it implies that scientific accounts are also loose. Until quite recently it was commonly held that science escaped the looseness of other empirical accounts. This belief provided a justification to put more confidence in science and technology than in other systems of knowledge. Religious faith, for instance, declined dramatically as science became more prominent. The looseness of scientific accounts undermines the unquestioning belief in science—it provokes a crisis of confidence. In recent years, science has been increasingly open to the challenge of justifying itself and increasingly subject to political decision making. In Chapter 5 we will review ethnomethodological research on this aspect of reflexivity.

It is not so obvious that every account is reflexive, regardless of its content. To understand how every account stands in a relationship with itself or acts upon itself, we must be very careful about the reference of an account—what it is about. I shall suggest that accounts do not more or less accurately describe things. Instead, they establish what is accountable in the setting in which they occur. Whether they are accurate or inaccurate by some other standard, accounts define reality for a situation in the sense that people act on the basis of what is accountable in the situation of their action. Later, if it becomes inconvenient to continue to act on some account, the content of what is accountable changes. For example, people drill wells when the probable presence of oil or water or gas underground justifies it. The accuracy of this account is ultimately judged by whether the well is successful or not. Regardless of the success of the well, however, the probable success is accountable, and it is that judgment that people act upon. At some point, if the well does not produce, people decide that the probable success of the well is not an accountable basis for action. They stop drilling. Drilling a well can be accountable when "in reality" there is nothing to drill for; stopping the drilling can be accountable when "in reality" a little additional effort will bring success. The account provides a basis for action, a definition of what is real, and it is acted upon so long as it remains accountable. *If men define things as real, the definitions are real in their consequences.* Whatever the content of an account, whatever it seems to be about, the effect of accounts is to provide a definition upon which action can be based. Accounts establish what people in a situation will believe, accept as sound, accept as proper—that is, they establish what is accountable.

I do not mean to imply that people, in attempting to establish what to believe, are aware of accountability as an issue. Nor do I mean to imply that, when people talk about things, they think they are defining them for the situation rather than attempting to reach the truth about them. Rather, this emphasis on establishing accountability as a socially ratified agreement about what to believe and act upon for the time being is an evaluation of what accounts accomplish from a researcher's perspective. We need to connect this assertion about the function of accounts with what the researcher actually observes. To that end, I will review some aspects of the study of categorizing juvenile offenders discussed in Chapter 1.

Cicourel observed that all participants in the legal system worked hard to establish the true character of the juvenile offenders and their families. They reasoned that the task of dealing with juveniles was to separate those who would continue to cause trouble from those who could be straightened out and to assign them to proper treatment. The nature of the offense was not so important in itself, but mostly for its reflection on the character of the juvenile. So, at each step in the official process, the files would be reviewed; the juvenile would be discussed with those who knew the case; attempts would be made to show the youth the danger of continuing to misbehave; signs of contrition were encouraged; the aid of the family was enlisted to supervise and discipline the youth; and so on. But the files that developed were not consistent, despite the seriousness of the efforts to establish the facts of the case. Different officials had different ideas of the character of the juveniles. As the case progressed, the fixing of responsibility and the understanding of the events changed. No effort was made to reconcile them in a final coherent package. When the same events were relevant to different cases, there was no effort to reconcile the contradictory versions of events reached in the various cases.

The key to understanding this approach to fact finding, even when everyone is serious and concerned with being accurate, is to place the investigation in the context of the practical decisions it supported. Each time a new official entered the case, each time the file was reinterpreted, the attempts to understand the case were undertaken in the process of making or justifying decisions. The practical question was always, "What should we do with this child?" The concern with the character of the child was instrumental to that decision. Whenever enough was known about the case and the child to support a plan of action, the inquiry stopped. In effect, the inquiry was concerned with defining events in as much detail as the practical problem required, *and no more.* In effect, the inquiry provided an accountable basis for action rather than a final truth about its content. In effect, the accounts establish what is accountable in the situation, not knowledge for general use. Each time the situation called for a decision, accounts would be assembled to justify a plan of action. Except as they compromised the current plan, accounts offered at other times were not interesting enough to correct, and no practical need existed to keep all the accounts consistent.

This characteristic of accounts is not limited to defining the characters of juveniles. The accounts of Agnes's gender also displayed inconsistency from occasion to occasion and incomplete investigation suited to the practical needs for which the investigation was undertaken. Even a doctor performing a physical examination for a job did not check Agnes carefully enough to discover her physical peculiarities. In some settings, the accounts of Agnes's gender justified treating her as a normal woman. In other settings the accounts of her gender justified treating her as a male child who had left home and returned looking like a female and drawing on family loyalty to exact treatment as a female from her family.

The people offering and accepting these various accounts of Agnes's gender believed, as far as we know, that her gender was a real, permanent, unchanging state of affairs. As far as we know, they were not cynical about their efforts to define it but, rather, believed that their accounts did not affect Agnes's gender and were approximations of an independent reality. In effect, though, these various accounts were Agnes's gender. At least they were her gender as it entered and influenced social relationships. In effect, each account of Agnes's gender established that gender as accountable for the situation in which it was accepted.

The variety of accounts is not the important issue. In each situation, people define a reality upon which they will act. They do so without expending more effort in the investigation than the action dictates. They do not work to be consistent with the definitions found in other settings. They do not reconsider all the evidence available in other settings to be sure of accuracy. A gender can be made accountable by no more than a gender-typed name such as Agnes. Leslie, Dale, and Pat do not work in the same way. By establishing what is accountable in each situation, people restrict their accounts, in effect, to local significance. So far as I know, my gender remains consistently male in all accounts of it. Still, since that gender must be made accountable in each setting, the accounts of gender still establish that gender as accountable *in a setting*. Consistent accounts are still not descriptions of their content; they still establish things as accountable rather than describe them. This becomes accountable to ethnomethodologists because they conduct research by doing exactly what is not normally done with accounts—they compare accounts from different settings and examine the evidence in more detail than the practical tasks of those settings require. The ethnomethodologists' practical task is to understand how accounts work, for which their detailed investigations are necessary.

Accounts, then, regardless of their subject matter, do not describe things. Rather, they establish what is accountable in the setting in which they occur. We shall now see that these settings are made up entirely of accounts. To understand this point, we will have to consider what else might be part of a social setting.

For most purposes, manufactured objects such as buildings, automobiles, garbage cans, chain saws, and disposable diapers can be conveniently understood to exist on their own, independent of our accounts of them. However, these objects are the products of considerable human activity. Each serves as an account of the activity that produced it, just as words on a page serve as an account. A disposable butane lighter is, in its plastic convenience, an account of considerable invention, marketing, distributing, exploring (for fuel), chemical engineering, and our way of life. We do not usually make this much of butane lighters, but I am only treating them in the same way as archeologists routinely treat the fire-making tools they uncover. A butane lighter, properly considered as an account of the activities that produced it and the uses to which it is put, tells as much about our way of life as chips of flint tell about our forebears'. Manufactured objects, then, serve as retrospective accounts of how and why they were produced and as prospective accounts of uses to which they can potentially be put. We simply treat the object as a medium of communication and decipher its message.

Objects that are not manufactured are treated in essentially the same way.

The only difference is that the information they provide was not encoded by humans. I have distinguished these objects from manufactured ones to make it clear that we can perceive decipherable messages in things and events that were not arranged for us by the actions of other people. Every human perception is manufactured, even if the perceived object is not. It is made by the very active process of seeing. We make things by perception as well as by manufacture.

Technically, then, we can view situations as made of our perceptions or accounts of objects rather than as the objects themselves. Things may exist independently of our accounts, but they have no human significance until they become accountable. Things may not exist, but they may take on human significance by becoming accountable. To understand how accounts work, we do not need to know what is true in some final sense. Rather, we need to know what is accountable or accepted as true. For example, we do not need to decide Agnes's true gender; we need to know how her gender is made accountable. What things really exist is an extremely important question. The more closely accounts approximate such real conditions, the better actions based on them will work. However, for the purpose of understanding the formal structure of accounts, we do not need to know what really exists. When people differ, we need not take sides.

We can now understand how every account is reflexive. Accounts establish what is accountable in a setting. At the same time, the setting is made up of those accounts. This reflexive relationship can be understood in two ways. If we think in terms of the definitions that are established through accounts, we can see that the accounts define reality and at the same time that they are that reality. If we think in terms of accountability, we can see that accounts establish what is accountable at the same time that they are the things that are accountable. Accounts are always in this reflexive relationship with themselves because they are the medium of definition and accountability and because they make up the defined, accountable world at the same time.

The theoretical importance of accounts and how they work is also clear. If social settings are made up entirely of accounts, then the processes by which accounts are offered and accepted are the fundamental social process. The formal structure of accounts is the fundamental social structure. This is exactly the position that Garfinkel has taken.

> In exactly the ways that a setting is organized, it *consists* of members' methods for making evident that setting's ways as clear, coherent, planful, consistent, chosen, knowable, uniform, reproducible connections— i.e., rational connections.
>
> Garfinkel (1967, p. 34)
>
> the activities whereby members produce and manage settings of organized everyday affairs are identical with members' procedures for making those affairs "account-able."
>
> Garfinkel (1967, p. 1)

Indexicality

Each account is part of the setting in which it occurs and which it helps organize. Reciprocally, each account is organized, in part, by the setting in which it occurs. The setting, remember, is itself made up entirely of accounts. The abstraction of one account from the rest eliminates information that contributes to the meaning of the abstracted account. In general, the participants in a social situation will have particular purposes, particular time references, particular resources available, and particular skills. All these matters, as we have seen, affect what will be accepted as an adequate account. These practical circumstances, and others, affect the meaning of accounts. Loose concepts take on a specific sense. Temporal references make some events meaningful, others irrelevant.

Consider the interactions between the police and the citizens of skid row. The police were inclined to allow vulgar familiarity and back talk from people on skid row without reprisal. However, when there was an audience, disrespect was likely to be punished by a display of police power, even arrest. The person's words and behavior in response to the police may have been the same on two occasions. Told to stop drinking and get off the street, the person may have insulted the police, responded slowly, and generally displayed disrespect. When no one was there to observe the performance, it was accepted without retribution. But, when others were present, the police responded forcefully. The same actions and words are a threat to authority on one occasion, a tolerable nuisance on another. The situation in which the episode occurs influences its meaning.

The term for influence of the setting on the meaning of accounts is *indexicality*.[7] Historically, indexicality has been considered only as a characteristic of linguistic accounts. An indexical expression is a linguistic expression that has different meanings on the different occasions on which it is used. The meaning of the expression may be quite clear on any occasion, but, when the expression is repeated, its meaning changes. For example, "It's raining" is an indexical expression. Its meaning is generally clear enough, but in different instances it refers to different times and different places. "I am hungry" is another indexical expression. The sentence refers to different times, places, and people on the various occasions of its use.

Indexical sentences are often clear in their meaning because supplementary information is communicated nonverbally when they are used. If everyone knows where he or she is and what time it is, the ambiguity of "It is raining" is greatly reduced. Similarly, when everyone knows who has said so, when, and where, the ambiguity of "I am hungry" is reduced. While their meaning is made clear by this contextual information, the indexicality of these sentences is not reduced. Ambiguity is not a necessary feature of indexical communication. The

[7] This discussion of indexicality draws most heavily from those of Bar-Hillel (1954) and Garfinkel and Sacks (1970).

crucial feature is the dependence of the meaning on its context. Often, the context makes the meaning quite clear. The topic for study is how people are able to use contextual information to achieve clarity and adequate reasoning for their purposes.

The meaning of indexical sentences varies in more consequential ways than just the identity of the speaker and the time and place of the utterance. "It's raining" has different meanings: on the day of a long awaited picnic, at the end of a drought, when the rivers are already overflowing their banks, or when one is driving and the temperature is near freezing. These variations are similar to the transformation of an insult from tolerable to unacceptable by the presence of an audience.

One of the major purposes of philosophy is to think, speak, and write clearly. A condition of success in those endeavors is precision in the use of language. Indexical expressions subvert those goals. The variability of their meaning may not cause trouble in ordinary discourse, although sometimes it does. But stripped of contextual information, as language is in written communication, indexical expressions are rendered more unclear.

Indexical expressions have been noted for over two thousand years by philosophers. "Loose concepts" are one kind of indexical expression, pronouns are another. These, and other kinds of indexical expressions, frustrate clear communication and the use of logic. Accordingly, indexical expressions have been addressed as a problem.

Indexical expressions have traditionally been contrasted to unproblematic, objective expressions. Objective expressions are clear and consistent in meaning, regardless of the nonlinguistic context in which they occur. Objective expressions will be understood to have the same reference by anyone who knows the language in which they are made. Mathematical formulations have this characteristic. Scientific reports are said to have it. The description of the research procedures gives a determinate sense to the results so long as the reader knows the specialized language employed and so long as all significant procedures are described.

Recently, the universality claimed for the meaning of objective statements has been broadened. We have begun to launch projectiles that will leave this solar system and to include messages in them which we hope will be understood by any beings who are intelligent enough to encounter the missiles. This sense of objectivity is not limited to those who share a language or even to members of a species. Our *Voyager* missiles, carrying images of us, mathematical notation, music, maps of our solar system, and, perhaps, coupons for special extraterrestrian rates at selected motels, mark the boundaries of our belief that a message can be completely self-contained. We are not hoping merely that an alien species will make something of the message; we are hoping that they will make the same of the message as we do. With luck, if they take offense they will not be able to decipher the maps.

Many approaches have been suggested to solve the problem posed by indexical expressions. In common, these approaches attempt to replace indexical expressions with objective ones and to justify a domain for precise linguistic expression. In scientific work, for example, looseness is a constant problem. The report of methodology and the development of precise measurement helps to reduce unclarity. The report of scientific research procedures is a special case of a general approach—expressing the nonlinguistic context of an expression linguistically. For example, tones of voice, the situation, and facial expressions can be described along with the words spoken.

The attempt to remedy indexical expressions tends to ignore the formal structure of ordinary language. Increased clarity may result, but, if the formal structure of accounts is different from that of traditional logic, the effort will never succeed completely. Also, this approach does not explain how indexical expressions are actually used in everyday life. In effect, approaching indexicality as a problem disregards what people actually do in favor of what they might do. Ordinary language is treated as having no distinctive formal structure. At its best, ordinary language approaches traditional logic in precision; at its worst, it is unclear and mistaken in its standards for argument. In either case, only logic and other rigorous formal systems are recognized as standards for adequate reasoning.

Garfinkel and Sacks describe this approach in a pleasant simile. Indexical expressions are like a spot of dirt on the white wall of language. For over two thousand years philosophers and scientists have unsuccessfully attempted to scrub the wall clean. For over two thousand years philosophers and scientists have debated how best to remove the blemish. (If I may embellish the simile, the treatment of indexicality is like a two-thousand-year-long series of commercials for various laundry products, each claiming to make the wall bright and clean.) Garfinkel and Sacks propose, instead, to examine that spot closely and to describe its characteristics. Perhaps, upon examination, the spot may prove to be a work of art. Ethnomethodologists are interested in the formal structure of commonsense accounts. To continue with the simile, they propose to put a frame around the spot and study it.

There is another fundamental difference between the ethnomethodological approach to indexicality and the traditional philosophical one. Philosophers define indexicality as a characteristic of linguistic expressions. Information is understood to be transmitted in other ways, tone of voice for example, but the information is treated as subordinate to linguistic expression and, generally, no formal structure is attributed to nonlinguistic expression. Ethnomethodologists consider indexicality as a formal characteristic of any account, regardless of the medium. For example, Agnes's urine sample is an *indexical particular*[8] whose

[8]   An indexical particular is anything that communicates meaning and communicates different meanings on different occasions. An indexical expression is a linguistic indexical particular.

meaning changes depending on the contextual knowledge of the person interpreting it. To the lab technician who analyzes it, it is just another urine sample;
to Agnes's roommate, it is a favor to a friend; to Agnes, it is a threat to discovery;
to us, it is an example of an indexical particular; to us, while reading Chapter 1,
it is an example of how perceptual routines can be manipulated. The linguistic
portion of accounts is not awarded special status in ethnomethodology, although
it is studied more. Any information, carried in any medium of communication,
is considered as an account. It is assumed to have the characteristic formal
structure of accounts; it is considered to have all other information as its context
and to be context for all other information. Any account is reflexive. Insofar as
it draws its meaning from its context, its meaning changes as the context changes.
Any account is indexical.

An exercise may help to bring this topic into focus for you. Think about
the various meanings of the phrase "It's raining." Imagine the various situations
I mentioned as clearly as you can, and, with your mind's ear, listen to the way
in which the words would be said on each occasion. Are the tones of voice,
inflections, volume, and so on interchangeable from situation to situation? How
would Joan of Arc say it? You know when. The tin man? Noah? Noah's next-
door neighbor? Notice the relationship among the words, the situation, the
nonverbal aspects of communication, and the meaning of the sentence. Now,
stop abusing your imaginations and listen carefully to people talking.

Let It Pass

"Let it pass" is a fundamental rule of accounting that Garfinkel (1967)
suggests is part of the formal structure of everyday accounts. By relating this
rule to reflexivity and indexicality and to the studies described in Chapter 1, we
can begin to see what is implied by "formal structure" and how ethnomethodologists attempt to study it. We begin with the axiomatic premise that any
account is only part of the total account of a situation. Every account is incomplete. Put another way, every account is technically loose or indexical.

In everyday life, people organize their conduct with reference to the
information available to them. This information is always incomplete and always
less than perfectly clear in the technical sense. It may, however, be quite satisfactory and cause no trouble. A persistent practical problem, then, is to make do
with indexical, more or less imprecise, accounts. Whenever people decide to act,
they will be acting on information that is imperfect from a technical standpoint.
People may be aware of inadequacies of their information from their own, nontechnical standpoint too. Sometimes information will seem adequate and people
will be confident in it, even though a technical analysis would show it to be
indexical. Sometimes, however, circumstances may compel action or information that appears inadequate and that is undertaken hesitantly or reluctantly.
These feelings about the information and the action based upon it are different

responses to data that are always technically indexical but vary in their value from other standpoints. Agnes, for example, needed to respond to a request for a urine sample without clear knowledge of what urinalysis could reveal about her. Her resources did not permit her to ascertain whether the risk of requesting a sample from her roommate was greater than the danger that she would be embarrassed by the analysis of her own urine. In so doing, Agnes was aware of the discrepancy between the knowledge available to her and the knowledge that she would prefer to act upon and let it pass. That is, she acted without seeking more knowledge.

"Let it pass" applies to steps in reasoning and to categorization. It provides that minor discrepancies be overlooked, at least temporarily. By letting it pass, people forgive each other minor disagreements over the applicability of loose concepts, the degree and nature of appropriate detail, and so on. Another's account is perceptibly imperfect in some way, but close enough to the account that one wanted to be accepted without undue complaint, at least temporarily. Later, new information may retroactively disqualify prior accounts. A teenage girl may be transformed from innocent victim to delinquent.

There are many reasons to let things pass, reflected in the many idioms in which the rule can be expressed. "You can't fight city hall." "Don't worry, its (I'm) insured." "Caveat emptor." "It's his (or her) life." "Everybody does it." "That's good enough for what they're paying." Application of this rule in any of its forms allows disagreements to be acknowledged as problems but still accepted as accountable reasoning for the time being. The person giving the account is temporarily forgiven slight deviations from one's expectations. Simultaneously, the person receiving the account is temporarily forgiven the failure to accept the account more enthusiastically. Each lets it pass. A person who does not let things pass may be regarded as uptight, grumpy, demanding, and a nuisance, although others may let that pass without too much trouble. Of course, if challenged too much, others can retaliate. To be social is to be forgiving.

The studies in Chapter 1 provide many illustrations of what can be involved in letting things pass. The doctors went to considerable pains to determine the truth of Agnes's condition when they were considering whether to perform her sex-change operation. But Agnes refused to let them interview her family, boyfriend, and others, and they ultimately decided to let her account pass as an adequate justification of surgery even though they wanted that information. Juvenile officers and the other authorities with whom they work do not attempt to reconcile the discrepancies in their various files. They let them all pass as adequate, even when it is apparent that they disagree with one another. Skid-row police allow disrespectful and illegal behaviors to occur openly unless there is a special reason to respond to them. The citizenry, for its part, does not strenuously challenge or resist inconsistencies in the application of these laws.

In all these settings, the people involved are able to maintain orderly social arrangements by forgiving accounts that are inconsistent, incomplete, or otherwise flawed from a technical standpoint. This practice and the constant reevaluation of situations as new information becomes available are part of the formal structure of accounts. It is studied by finding ways in which accounts are technically imperfect and then observing the conditions under which the accounts remain acceptable anyway, the troubles caused by acting on incomplete accounts, and the resolution of those troubles. Instead of a fixed standard of acceptable information such as the law of the excluded middle used in technical arguments, practical circumstances are managed by using information judged by flexible standards, often with little confidence. To let it pass is to apply those standards.

ANTECEDENTS TO THE ETHNOMETHODOLOGICAL APPROACH

The substance of the ethnomethodological approach and its terminology have been influenced by earlier attempts to incorporate fundamental implications of indexicality and reflexivity in social theory. The work of Alfred Schutz on the attitude of everyday life or commonsense attitude and Karl Mannheim on the documentary method of interpretation have been the most strikingly influential. Although modifications have been made, ethnomethodological imagery and terminology are greatly indebted to Mannheim and Schutz.

The Commonsense Attitude[9]

Alfred Schutz, a phenomenologically oriented social philosopher, had considerable influence on the development of ethnomethodological thought. He argued that people can adopt different attitudes or different sets of assumptions about the world. Each attitude leads to the experience of a distinctive reality, and each includes a distinctive formal structure. The commonsense attitude, also called the natural attitude or the attitude of everyday life, is Schutz's model of the attitude of adult humans as they pursue practical affairs. Its characteristic form of reasoning is the use of indexical expressions, which Schutz calls typifications. This term indicates that all categorizations and inferences have typicality as the standard of adequacy, not the precision of traditional logic.

The foundation of commonsense reasoning is the unquestioned belief that the world really exists and has characteristics that are imposed on us indepen-

---

[9]   This discussion of Schutz is based primarily on Schutz (1964; 1967).

dently of our definitions of it. Fire burns. Speed kills. When confusion arises, when events appear ambiguous, the commonsense belief is that there is some determinate truth to the matter. The confusion or ambiguity is a failure of knowledge and can be resolved by investigation. In the commonsense world, there is continual interest in clarification, in reducing ambiguity. But this interest stands against a background of an unquestioned belief that answers can always be found if the question is addressed properly. The world exists and its existence is not questioned. The world has characteristics that are imposed on us. These characteristics must be discovered by investigation, not defined arbitrarily. The belief in the stubborn reality of the world guarantees that answers can be found to any question about it.

In the commonsense attitude, the world is always addressed from practical motivation. The world is, in part, a condition of action. To achieve one's ends, one must correctly identify the unalterable characteristics of the world and accommodate action to them. To some extent, the world is manipulatable and provides resources for action. The presence of an ocean between the United States and Europe is a condition of any action designed to move a person from one to the other. Gravity is another inflexible feature of the situation. However, we can build planes and boats.

In the commonsense attitude, definitions of events are judged to be better or worse. The criterion for judgment is the success of plans based on those definitions. As plans unfold in action, continuous minor imperfections lead to continuous minor adjustments of our definitions. It is characteristic of the commonsense attitude that one is not shaken in one's belief in a determinate world by the continuous, if minor, failure of our comprehension. It is also characteristic of common sense to communicate one's understandings to others with the premise that disagreements will be resolved by exposure to the common reality. Differences in perceiving and defining events are attributed to differences in purpose and perspective. Disagreements with others about the nature of events do not shake the commonsense belief in their imposed reality.

Neither imperfections in one's own definitions nor disagreements with others are corrected for the sake of perfect understanding. They are corrected only as they cause problems for the successful completion of one's plans. The belief that correct understanding can be achieved is not tested. Instead, one is concerned only that definitions are close enough to accuracy so that one's plans will work satisfactorily. The issue is not precision of thought for its own sake but, rather, practical success. And practical success is not judged against the harsh criterion of perfection; instead, it is judged by the practical criterion of being not worth the trouble to improve. Ethnomethodologists use the term "objective (adequate) for the purpose at hand (all practical purposes)" to describe knowledge that meets this practical criterion. As the purpose changes, knowledge may be transformed from adequate to inadequate, or vice versa.

The Documentary Method of Interpretation[10]

Mannheim was concerned with understanding social scientific knowledge from a social scientific perspective. That is, he was concerned with the reflexivity of social scientific statements. Specifically, he was concerned with understanding the interpretation and reinterpretation of historical events by historians of different periods and by historians of different political persuasions during a given period. You can see what concerned Mannheim for yourself without extensive research. Look at history books used in public schools with publication dates scattered over a thirty- or forty-year period and see what each has to say about a major event. The writing will be simple and the presentations brief, but even over such a short period of time you will find wide variation in attitudes toward the American Indian, the various waves of immigration, the Civil War, or what have you.

Mannheim argued that these changes of interpretation are essential to cultural and social scientific knowledge, but not to natural scientific knowledge. They occur, he suggested, because cultural and social scientific knowledge is different in kind from knowledge in the natural sciences and is apprehended in a different way. His concern was to characterize the formal structure of cultural and scientific knowledge, which he called documentary, and to consider how it is achieved and defended.

Mannheim argued that *documentary knowledge* is knowledge of the patterns that underlie behavior. Individual items—patterns of behavior, works of art, religious beliefs—serve as evidence or documents of the underlying patterns. For example, each work of art is a document of the overall meaning of an artist's work. Documentary patterns may be more or less complex and encompassing. The most encompassing of these patterns is the *Weltanschauung* or "world view" of an era. It encompasses the entire social and cultural reality of an historical period. The pattern can be discovered only by reflection upon all of the less encompassing patterns of the period—the style and substance of art and literature, etiquette, fashion, patterns of conduct, the issues of political life, patterns of social inequality, religious beliefs, scientific achievement, and so on. The more immersed one becomes in these documents of the era, the more completely can one grasp and formulate the spirit of the time. Reciprocally, once the pattern is grasped, it lends meaning to the less encompassing documents. For example, by looking at many paintings, one can grasp what the "Pop Art" movement was about. Once the pattern is grasped, each painting takes on meaning from its place in the pattern.

Mannheim suggested that there are three kinds of knowledge: objective, expressive, and documentary. *Objective knowledge* is knowledge of the meaning

---

[10]   This discussion is based primarily on Mannheim (1964).

of things from a taken for granted perspective of the era. For example, in our era, the objective meaning of authors' appearing on a series of local television and radio shows is that they are publicizing their books and promoting sales. *Expressive knowledge* is knowledge of what the actor subjectively intends to express in his or her conduct. On a promotional tour, it often appears that authors intend to express their concern for issues, commitment to an educational mission, their own brilliance, or the special quality or utility of their work. These are among the subjective meanings of their conduct, whether they succeed in communicating the intended message or not. The world view of the period serves as global background that allows both these interpretations to be made. It is by knowing the facts about promotional tours in our era that particular tours are recognized for what they are. It is by knowing patterns of self-expression in our era that we can grasp the intended messages.

Mannheim wanted to make this global pattern an object of scientific study. Instead of merely living in an era and intuitively sharing its perspective, he argued that students of society must formulate this perspective. They must come to know it explicitly. But a paradox arises. The perspective of an era intuitively grasped affects how items will be interpreted. This creates a special relationship between the documentary pattern displayed in a collection of items and the items. One's own intuitive grasp of one's own era influences the items to which one will attend and what one will make of them. Thus, the global perspective helps to create the documents that are employed as evidence in explicating the global perspective. One's place in the social structure—one's education, class status, income, religion, and so on—serve to influence one's grasp of the global perspective. Thus, documentary interpretation will vary with one's social position. It will also vary as one passes through different stages of the life cycle. The diverse documentary interpretations are documents of the era in which they occur. So, for example, the interpretation of their own era, and others, by medieval historians, is an important document of the nature of the medieval era. And the sense we make of that document is a document of our own era.

Book promotion through television interviews seems to document the importance of television as an arbiter of taste, especially with respect to mass marketing. Authors and their books are at one with doctors and their diet plans, psychologists and their sex and child-rearing advice, sellers and their records, acne medication, and kitchen tools, consumer advocates, and hucksters of diverse products and corporate images. Whether they pay for the exposure as an acknowledged advertisement or present themselves as newsworthy, all need television to create a market and all must accommodate themselves to its format and substantive restrictions. Perhaps in a few years, we will be less impressed with the importance of television to this period of time and draw new conclusions about these practices, and others. Notice that the proposed documentary meaning does not imply that authors recognize or intend their kinship to actors in laxative commercials. Some do; some don't.

Mannheim's methodological suggestions are sketchy. To probe the documentary meaning of events in an era, one must attend to as many items as possible, grasp and express the pattern they display, and then test one's comprehension by attending to additional items suggested by the explicated pattern. The goal is to make a statement that encompasses as many items as possible. The importance of Mannheim's discussion to ethnomethodology lies more in his recognition of the reflexivity and indexicality of social knowledge than in the adequacy of his methodological suggestions.

Ethnomethodologists have applied the documentary method of interpretation to a different domain. Mannheim was concerned primarily with the interpretation of global cultural patterns. His temporal reference was the passage of historical eras and within each era his contextual concerns were with the overall structural arrangement of society. He did acknowledge, however, that the formal structure of documentary interpretation was also exhibited in the interpretation of the relatively faster and less encompassing events of face-to-face social interaction. Ethnomethodologists have made these relatively quick, small activities their major concern.

The justification of this diminution of scale is relatively simple. Mannheim was concerned with defining events as they appeared from the perspective of an era. However, every attempt to define events from the perspective of an era would be, in fact, a definition of those events from the perspective of an era at a particular moment during the era and from a particular practical standpoint. No matter how extensive the research, ultimately, the account is constructed in a particular situation of relatively short duration. We have already seen examples of this in the attempt to define events in the relatively short histories of problem juveniles. This does not imply that extensive research is unnecessary; only that the facts must be understood as they are assembled in a particular situation and that they must be understood to change from situation to situation. Claiming that the facts are valid, relevant, coherent, and credible over an extended period of time and in many situations does not alter the fact that their validity, relevance, coherence, and credibility are established in each situation for its duration and for its purposes.

WHY ETHNOMETHODOLOGY IS SO ABSTRACT

It should have become apparent by now, that ethnomethodologists discuss data that are picayune. Ethnomethodologists are quite seriously interested in the meaning of urine samples and how that meaning is achieved, the response of beat police officers to snide remarks, the observation that simple phrases change meaning from occasion to occasion, and so on. But these matters are considered in terms of highly abstract issues. So abstract are the issues, in fact, that ethnomethodologists most frequently attempt to conduct empirical research on topics ordinarily treated as matters for philosophical discussion. Instead of leaving logic to logicians, for example, ethnomethodologists treat logic as a substantive theory of reasoning and are attempting to improve upon it by empirical research.

A moment's reflection will indicate why this schism between the extreme concreteness of the data and the extreme abstraction of the sense made of them is necessary. Accounting occurs everywhere and always. I mentioned, for example, that primitive social groups do not have petroleum in their environments, even when, by our accounts, it is in the ground under them. Still, they are accounting, making sense, in the same way as we are. The factual evidence they accept is different, and this difference is important in many ways. But it is not important to the study of how accounting is done with the facts at hand. If I wanted to say something that is true of all professional football teams, I should have to ignore quite a few differences among them, searching for the common features. If I limited my search to NFL teams, my task would be reduced. If I expanded my interests to all professional athletic teams, I should have to abstract my common features from among still more variations. Ethnomethodologists are interested in constructing an account that encompasses the common features of all situations in which humans make sense. They are attempting, after all, to study the process of reasoning itself. This process will have to be abstracted from situations as diverse as winos' arranging proper turns on a wine bottle and bankers' attempting to project housing values in the various neighborhoods in a city. There are many differences to be disregarded for this purpose. What remains will be highly abstract.

SUMMARY

Categorization and inference display a formal structure. Insofar as not every categorization will be accepted as accurate and not every inference will be accepted as valid, people act as if there are rules for making sense. In their own reasoning, oriented to the successful achievement of practical goals, people attempt to reason and categorize accurately. They judge the reasoning of others, as well, and attempt to reconcile differences of opinion through communication.

Traditional logic has been utilized as the model for this reasoning process for over two thousand years, although the details of the model have been modified from time to time. By all accounts, it has been a very successful theory of reasoning. However, the model is not without its difficulties. Empirical terms are problematically accommodated by traditional logic. This difficulty has been recognized for almost as long as the model has existed, and without an acceptable remedy. Adequate descriptions of events are easily demonstrated to be a function of temporal reference and, in turn, a function of the practical circumstances under which the events are described. The question of "What happened?" has no single answer.

These formal difficulties have been addressed, typically, under the assumption that traditional logic is the proper model for reasoning. Where common usage does not seem to fit the model, common usage is held to be erroneous, sloppy, careless, and so on. But the assumption that traditional logic must be the model of everyday reasoning need not go unchallenged. The premises of traditional logic are axiomatic, accepted without question or proof. Alternative axioms are already available, although none seem more appropriate to the reasoning of everyday life.

Ethnomethodological thought begins with the premise that a new formal structure of accounts is a prerequisite to understanding human activities. Two fundamental commitments have been made as premises for research. All accounts are reflexive. All accounts are indexical. The goal is to explicate a formal structure that respects these principles. The principles are formalizations of the variety of problems encountered when traditional logic is applied to everyday reasoning.

A number of terms were introduced. Reflexivity refers to the premise that all accounts are part of the situation that they organize. Indexicality is the dependence of an account upon the context in which it occurs for its meaning. The attitude of everyday life is the orientation of people who are engaged in practical activities. It is a partial specification of the rules for using indexical expressions. The documentary method of interpretation is another term for the formal structure of activities involved in understanding indexical expressions. It stresses the reciprocal influence of inference and evidence upon one another. The reciprocal influence of one's social circumstances and one's social knowledge is a special case of this.

A FORMAL EXERCISE

This exercise is an extension of the first. Go out and observe people interacting when you are not part of the interaction. Do not invade privacy. Go to a public place and pay attention. Watch. Listen. Take notes about a few episodes in as much detail as you can. Episodes may be as brief as two people greeting one another in passing. Bring your notes to class and proceed as in the first exercise. Do this while the episodes are still fresh in your mind and can be filled in from memory when you are questioned.

The goal of this exercise is to improve your ability to take notes. Attend closely to what you and others must add to your notes from memory. In taking notes for a more extended project, there will be many entries dispersed over a long time period. Memory will fail. Repeat this exercise a few times until your notes are adequate.

SUGGESTED READINGS

You should be able to tackle any of the three studies discussed in Chapter 1. They pose two challenges. First, you will need to become accustomed to the jargon they employ. Second, you should try to identify examples of the conceptual issues raised in Chapter 2 in addition to the ones I have mentioned.

Of the philosophical discussions reviewed in Chapter 2, Carroll's is, of course, the best written. Conceptually, however, it is the one most completely discussed in this book and therefore the one from which you will learn least. Black (1970a) is quite clearly argued relative to the other technical papers and provides an excellent discussion of loose or indexical expressions and their implications. Garfinkel and Sacks (1970) is very difficult but very important. I'd recommend attempting to read it later, after you have read more of this book and a couple of empirical studies. Mannheim (1964) and Schutz (1964; 1967) are mainly of historical importance. Mannheim's paper is difficult, but very impressive. Williams (1977) provides an excellent discussion of questioning the reality of things and the grounds for continuing to believe in them.

3

An
Illustrated Program:
Practical Reasoning
or
the Commonsense
Attitude

We're after formal structures, the structures of everyday life.

Now, you, one and all, have navigated in the world of everyday life every day of your lives. Chances are, you are now, or have been, a college student. You've probably been exposed to a variety of formal systems—algebra, for one, the calculus for another. Perhaps you've taken a required course in logic or an elective one. You are being told that events in your everyday life are ordered differently from events in the other systems you have learned. Why haven't you noticed? And why, whatever its structure, aren't you aware of the structure of everyday life? Certainly, you've no lack of experience from which to abstract.

THE BLIND SPOT
OF THE COMMONSENSE ATTITUDE

Taking an attitude excludes some topics from consideration. Originally, the term attitude referred to the posture and position of the body, especially when they communicated anticipated action. A student who maintains alert facial expressions, unslumped posture, and poised readiness to write is striking the attitude of the interested, alert student. (Sneak a look at your colleagues in some dull class. I believe you will see this attitude struck despite awesome odds against its sincerity.) The notion of an attitude as a state of mind or mental orientation is an extension of our understanding of what it means to be ready for a particular line of conduct—to be poised for action.

Striking an attitude prepares one to perceive and think in particular ways, too. To strike the attitude of the intelligent, alert student, one must look in a particular direction, although occasional staring into space is also permitted, especially if followed by a flurry of writing. By looking in one direction, one foregoes interesting sights in others. For example, to see your fellow students striking this attitude, you must watch them. That will require your turning your head and displaying interest in their direction. In short, you will have to look away from the instructor and forego the attitude of the alert student for a while. Two things are important about this: (1) each attitude directs attention to some matters and excludes it from others, and (2) the exclusion is actively achieved and preserved. Attention to some matters is achieved by diverting attention from others.

The commonsense attitude and other mental orientations also actively distribute attention. The commonsense, or natural, attitude is defined, in part, by its characteristic commitment of attention to some matters and exclusion of attention from others. The direction of attention is accomplished through routines of perception. So long as the routine is undisturbed and the attitude unchanged, the excluded matters are not noticed. They cannot be noticed because the routines of perception restrict the availability of evidence. The natural attitude, then, renders some topics chronically uninteresting. People in the natural attitude do not notice these matters; they are not interested in noticing them; they will resist restructuring their attention, even when these matters are pointed out.

What are these topics? What does common sense exclude from attention? Generically, they are things that no one with a lick of common sense is interested in. Nonetheless, many find them interesting. Among the many are ethnomethodologists.

Assumptions are crucial to the maintenance of routines of perception. They predispose one to interpret ambiguous events in harmony with one's presumptions.[1] Assumptions, when acted upon, often create the conditions that one already assumed to have existed. This is often referred to as "self-fulfilling prophecy."[2] Assumptions encourage one to restrict the scope and nature of inquiry. Thus, assumptions reduce the availability of information that might contradict them. After all, there is no point in investigating what one already knows.

A bat assumes that today, as on a lifetime of yesterdays, its route through the bat cave will be unchanged. It acts on that assumption. It does not employ its sonar, thus restricting the channels open to contrary information. Millions of years of evolution weigh in favor of this approach; experimenters with 2 X 4s weigh against it. Physicians assume that males have penises and that females do not. Agnes's conduct during her physical examination was apparently never considered as evidence concerning this empirical matter. She may have been regarded as strange by the doctors, but not strange because she was a woman with a penis. Skid-row police assume that the people on their beats are unreliable and lead unstructured, unpredictable lives. Accordingly, they do not attempt to quickly locate people in whom they are interested. Instead, they keep several interests in mind, pursue their own rounds in their own order, and happen upon people whenever their paths cross. By conducting themselves in this way, the police preclude discovering that, to the contrary, skid-row dwellers are easy to find. In general, when things are taken for granted, the recognition of alternatives is reduced or precluded.

Among the presumptions protected from scrutiny within the attitude of everyday life is the taken for granted formal structure of that attitude. One cannot scrutinize the attitude of everyday life as an object while holding the

[1]　Fascinating empirical studies of this aspect of assumptions have been reported by Haire (1968), Hastorf and Cantril (1968), Wittreich (1968), and Toch and Schulte (1968).

[2]　Shibutani (1973) discusses an interesting case of this phenomenon. Schelling (1979) discusses a variety of ways in which initial individual attitudes are acted upon, creating a social environment of action for others.

attitude of everyday life. That is why, while pursuing one's everyday rounds in a commonsense way, none of us notices these matters. The dynamics of this routine of perception are very important to understanding ethnomethodology.

Consider the assumption that the world has real characteristics that are imposed on us independently of our knowledge of them. We assume of these characteristics that they partially compel our perception but also that error, distortion, and bias are possible in our understanding. Recognizing that error is possible permits us to reconsider particular bits of knowledge without considering the accuracy of our assumption that the world has real characteristics. The recognition of error suggests an explanation for differences of opinion, changes of mind, perceptions that do not support successful action, and so on. The perception or thinking was faulty. Assume instead that the stubborn, real characteristics of the world fully compel our perception. Assume that we do and must see what is there. Then, even one contradiction would raise the possibility that the world is a chimerical will o' the wisp or nothing at all beyond what we make of it. Thus, the ontological assumptions of the commonsense attitude protect themselves from scrutiny. There is no implication here that they are incorrect, simply that the combination of them reduces inquiry into their own nature and accuracy. The assumptions make a certain kind of world available to scrutiny; the assumptions are not part of that world.

In the commonsense attitude, "typicality" and "close enough for the purposes at hand" are the unquestioned standards of judgment. Disagreements that are too trivial to affect practical interests are dismissed as uninteresting, even if they are noticed. They are errors not worth correcting. Such errors are not further investigated. Attempts to be more precise than necessary to achieve an acceptable level of success in a situation are resisted. They are nit-picking, a waste of time. Forgiving minor errors and discrepancies makes the rules of judgment invisible. No attention is paid to the necessary data. In addition, these standards of accuracy reduce the need to question particular factual matters by rendering many disagreements uninteresting. This reduces challenges to the ontological assumptions.

In the commonsense attitude, the world is always considered in terms of practical motives. The world cannot be addressed indifferently. Knowledge is not pursued for its own sake, with no particular practical motive. Thus, so long as the commonsense attitude works well enough for the purposes at hand, it cannot be investigated in a commonsense way. Imagine what a failure of the commonsense attitude would be like. Our courses of action would have to fail consistently and fail in ways that offer no reasonable explanation. Our perceptions would have to become recognizably untrustworthy. We might find ourselves in chronic and irreparable disagreement with others. We might find our circumstances so strange and disorderly that we must doubt our very way of looking at them. If such a state of affairs came to pass, people might become so confused and so in need of practical solutions to their situation that they stop trying to perceive and reason and begin to consider how they perceive and reason.

Consider the dimensions of this carefully. A major earthquake shakes the ground, causes landslides, makes up down, starts fires, destroys roads and bridges, disrupts food and medicine and water supplies, and limits communication. Rivers jump their banks; they flow in the wrong direction. Earthquakes ruin one's day, for sure. But they are not disorienting in a way that brings attention to the commonsense attitude as an object of practical interest. People do not know what to do. They do not know when their lives will become routinized again or on what basis. They are often financially ruined. Families are decimated. But people in such circumstances know what is happening. It is an earthquake. The uncertainty is explicable. What they do not know—first aid, how to test water, why them, and so on—is simple ignorance. The environment has turned nasty, but not senseless. The commonsense attitude does not easily become an object of practical concern.

A special motive, an interest outside our normal practical concerns, is needed to make everyday reasoning processes an interesting object of study. But the motive will not be a practical one, and the motives of the commonsense attitude are all practical ones. To make the formal structure of the commonsense attitude interesting as an object of study, we must take a different attitude.

Fortunately, there are other attitudes from which to choose. To understand how thoroughly a transformation of one's fundamental attitude transforms experience, let's consider the attitude of the theater (Schutz 1967). When one attends a play or movie or watches television, one observes people performing comprehensible human acts on the stage or screen. But these acts are not experienced as they are in real life. We do not experience an actor's experience of grief as an expression of his or her own feelings. At best, we experience them as an expression of the character's feelings. We are not in mortal fear of an actor on stage who brandishes a weapon and acts in a homicidal or deranged manner. We do not believe the weapon is real. And yet we accept that the weapon kills other characters on the stage. But it is the characters who are dead, not the actors. We do not expect that the proclamations of a stage president will be enacted into law. And yet we accept that the other characters on stage act as if they are. Fairies appear; children fly; people turn into rhinoceroses. We watch. The theater is a different reality from the reality of the commonsense world.

Similarly, we do not expect our dream experiences to have the same relevance in our workaday lives as do our waking experiences. We do not expect our dreams to be ordered like the working world or bound by its strictures. Dreams are another reality, constituted by a different attitude.

The attitude appropriate to the task of making the attitude of common sense interesting as an object of study is called the attitude of *scientific theorizing* (Schutz 1967). The phrase "attitude of scientific theorizing" is often abbreviated to "scientific attitude," but the novice is well served to remember that this attitude more resembles the reflective reasoning of analytic philosophy than the workings of empirical science. Empirical science, remember, involves loose concepts. Schutz characterizes the scientific attitude in terms of three postulates. These are quite different from the assumptions of the commonsense attitude and create a different formal structure.

The first postulate of the scientific attitude is a *commitment to logical consistency*. In the attitude of scientific theorizing, clarity and precision of thought and expression are ends in themselves. The theorist is held to rigorous logic as a standard of argument and, of course, to use no loose concepts.

The second postulate is the postulate of *subjective interpretation*. Human action must be understood in terms of its meaning or the meaning of its results to the actors involved. The theorist is not held to a course of psychological investigation in which the thoughts of each participant in a social event are determined. Instead, the theorist is held to construct a model of the actor, endowed with specified thoughts, motives, and so on. The behavior is explained subjectively when the model is constructed in such a way that people, endowed subjectively as the model is endowed, would act as they actually do. To explain why people eat, we endow the model of the actor with hunger; to explain why people buy tickets to football games and then stay home, we endow them with the desire to see the home games on television and some motive to be willing to be the ones who pay for tickets and create the "sellout"; or we endow them with the flu; and so on.

The third postulate, the postulate of *adequacy*, sets the standard for evaluating the model of the actor. When the model of the actor is adequately constructed, it must be possible to predict courses of action that would be undertaken by a person endowed only as the model is endowed. These courses of action must be comprehensible to people as correct ones within their commonsense perspective. That is, a person instructed to act solely as the theorist predicts would act acceptably in the commonsense world. A robot, programmed to act as the theorist instructs, would pass for human, assuming that the problem of appearance could be overcome. Some robots already play mean games of chess, read handwriting, converse with chimpanzees, teach children in school, and serve miserable coffee while making change. Still, there is a long way to go.

If one adopts these three postulates and examines everyday life, one's attention is drawn immediately to its formal structure as an object of study. That formal structure will be strikingly interesting to one committed to logic and clarity. The ways in which logic and clarity are disappointed in everyday talk and action will be immediately encountered as a problem and later as a topic of study. First, there will be difficulty in using everyday language clearly. Second, it will become crucial to understand how language and action are structured in everyday life to construct a model of the actor. Without a precise rendering of everyday reasoning, an adequate model of the actor, especially one that includes the actor's subjectivity, will be impossible. Thus, for the purpose of scientific theorizing, it will not do to repair indexical expressions as they arise. This may clarify one's own expression, but it will not contribute to the model of the actor.

The program of ethnomethodology, then, although expressed in various ways, involves adopting this scientific attitude and making rigorously logical statements about the formal structure of everyday life. As you shall soon see, putting this program into practice was influenced greatly by the belief that the commonsense attitude resists scrutiny.

BREACHES, ETC.

Rationale

The breaches[3] are a series of ingenious demonstrations of some formal characteristics of the commonsense attitude and of the activities involved in sustaining the sense of everyday events. The commonsense attitude conceals itself from observation. To make people aware of their own sense-making activities and to make those activities the topic of discussion, the commonsense attitude must be disturbed. Sense-making activities occur ceaselessly, but they become most evident to an observer when assumptions about the world are proved inadequate. A person sitting in a chair watching treetops shimmer in the wind is engaged in making sense of his or her environment. That observer provides poor data, however. Aside from an occasional squint, that person's accounting activities are covert. To improve the data, the person must be encouraged to talk about his or her thoughts, to think aloud. Thinking aloud about the thinking process itself would be even better data, but to obtain them the person must be motivated to think about that process. Hence we need a disturbance of some kind to breach the attitude of common sense. This approach assumes that the accounting activities that become evident during the period of disturbance are formally identical to those occurring covertly the rest of the time.

Obviously, the breaches are not created by massive disruptions of the environment, disruptions so severe that the attitude of common sense comes under scrutiny as a last resort. Committees on the treatment of human subjects would never put up with it. Instead, using prior, rough knowledge of the attitude of everyday life, substantively minor disturbances are designed specifically to produce a senseless environment. Thus, a small disruption, arranged so that sense-making repairs will not work to correct it, produces attention to sense-making activities without dramatic manipulations. The accounting activities of the subjects of the breaches can then be studied to refine our knowledge of their formal structure. As a matter of fact, if not necessarily prior design, increasing

---

[3]   The breaches are discussed primarily in Garfinkel (1963; 1964; 1967).

refinement of our knowledge and sensitivity to how to observe accounting activities make the intentional creation of breaches unnecessary in later studies.

The Disturbances

The disturbances have two common features. First, an ordinary social activity is changed in some way so that expectations are violated. This engenders attempts to reestablish a sense of order. Second, the attempts to normalize the situation are systematically frustrated so that the efforts to normalize the situation become problematic in themselves. When attention is turned from the disrupted social scene to the failure of efforts to normalize it, the commonsense attitude has been breached. In Garfinkel's (1964, p. 227) phrase, the experimenter "multiplies the senseless features of the perceived environment."

What Do You Mean?   This breach is accomplished by refusing to accept clear colloquial usage without explanation. Perfectly obvious idiomatic expressions are taken literally. Taken literally, they are ambiguous, and, instead of understanding their idiomatic sense, people are challenged to explain them more fully. For example,

(S) Hi, Ray. How is your girlfriend feeling?

(E) What do you mean, how is she feeling? Do you mean physical or mental? (Garfinkel, 1964, p. 230)

One continues to converse in this manner, obstinately refusing to understand what is said by the other. Anger is produced along with the suspicion that something is seriously wrong.

The presence of anger and the imputation that the obstinate experimenter is acting in a disturbed manner are the keys to interpreting this breach. People do not merely become confused when their remarks are not understood. Nor do they take it upon themselves to clarify their remarks endlessly. Instead, they expect their remarks to be understood and they hold others accountable to understand them. Hence, anger and recrimination. The indexical character of everyday talk is shown to be an enforceable, accountable right as well as a matter of fact. This infusion of indexicality with moral accountability shows another way in which the commonsense attitude defends itself from scrutiny. People claim it as a moral right to remain in that attitude and to require others to do likewise. People let things pass. They also feel normatively required to do so and they require it of others.

The Boarders (Garfinkel 1964).   Two related breaches were arranged by having students pretend to be boarders in their own homes. In the first experiment, students were assigned to spend from fifteen minutes to an hour at home viewing activities as a boarder would. As more and more routine events required reinterpretation, the time constraint prevented reestablishing the scene's normal sense. Students were specifically told not to act as boarders in this experiment. In the second experiment, students were told to act as boarders in their own homes. Specifically, they were "instructed to conduct themselves in a circumspect and polite fashion. They were to avoid getting personal, to use formal address, to speak only when spoken to" (Garfinkel 1964, p. 232). It is doubtful, and irrelevant, whether or not these instructions could be derived from an adequate model of a boarder. It is also irrelevant whether or not the students could see events in their own homes as a real boarder would. The only issue was to make the environment senseless. Certainly, following these instructions in an intimate setting would produce behavior that would appear strange to the other participants. Persisting in the behavior would produce a breach.

In the reports of their observations as covert boarders, the students behaviorized what they saw. That is, they tried not to draw on their prior knowledge of family members and family life and to describe only what was physically before them, without filling in remembered details. Thus, events were described without detail provided by historical knowledge of the relationships. In attempting to not use their personal knowledge of the scene, the students apparently disregarded their general cultural knowledge as well. Thus, a man entered the room, kissed people in greeting, read the paper, discussed the days events, and laughed at a woman's joke during dinner. But he was not identified as husband and father to those present, although a stranger would probably have inferred that relationship from the scene, even without personal familial knowledge.

Here, I think, the particularistic character of everyday scenes is evident. One's own family has a history, relationships, habits. One's own family is not an instance of families, not a minor variation on typical themes. Deprived by experimental design of the true commonsense facts of the case, the students did not substitute other knowledge. If people, in general, are reluctant to substitute one body of background knowledge for another, preferring to think of one body of knowledge as the uniquely appropriate one for understanding the case at hand, the flexibility of interpretation would be reduced. This ought to normalize the world of one's experience and, when acted upon, provide an orderly world for others. It should also protect the formal structure of the knowledge from scrutiny.

The estrangement brought attention to events in the home that students had previously not noticed. The students became uncomfortably aware of the details of ordinary behavior: how people greeted one another, how silverware was handled. Bickering and hostility, usually unnoticed when contrasted to the detailed knowledge of warm family relationships, became annoyingly apparent. Several students reported the facts but also reported that the stranger's eye view seemed to produce an inaccurate version of activities. And so it should. The indexical activities cannot make their usual sense without references to their usual context. The sense of inaccuracy is a sign that the students had become aware that the way in which one looks at a situation affects what is seen.

Several additional points must be made about this breaching exercise. First, it demonstrates clearly that an unusual motive can transform the way in which events are perceived by affecting the way in which background information is employed. Second, the unusual motive and the peculiar experience it supports can be easily concealed from others with whom one interacts. Third, unusual motives can be adopted and abandoned at will, although they may also be thrust upon one. Finally, even when one's motive is eminently practical, as is completing a course assignment, it is disturbing if the motive does not permit one to sustain the sense that he or she is sharing an understanding of the environment with others. This disorientation occurs even when one continues to interact with others in the usual way but accounts to oneself, privately, in an odd manner.

The group of students who were assigned to act as boarders had even rougher sledding. The exercise was assigned to forty-nine students, five of whom would not do it. Two families treated the strange behavior as a joke; two families noticed it but were unconcerned. The remaining forty families became anxious and angry to various degrees. Students were charged with being inconsiderate, nasty, selfish, of having gone crazy, of having a serious problem. In short, the altered behavior produced the same sort of angry responses as the refusal to understand idiomatic speech.

Habitual styles of interaction were asserted by the families as their moral due. The disruption of habit produced anger and resentment, reactions that closely resembled sanctions for the violation of group norms. When the students explained that their behavior had been experimental, the families were not mollified. Apparently, violations of the families' rights to be treated in the habitual way required a better excuse than a class assignment. When the students explained that they had been playing an assigned role and did not mean what they had said and done, the families did not disregard the offensive conduct. They continued to wonder how much of the behavior had been feigned and how much the student had really meant. In effect, the students were denied their requests for a "time out" from moral obligations to act in the ways expected of them. The families apparently experienced the same difficulty as the passive boarders did when asked to interpret events without using the usual body of background information. In their anger we can see that the orientation of conduct to the habitual context is defended as a moral right.

These angry reactions should exert a conservative influence on relationships by discouraging disturbances of routine, habitual interaction. But note that it is the maintenance of the routine, whatever its character, that is defended, and only incidentally the particular habits that constitute the relationships. The effect, then, is for the commitment to honoring routines as a moral obligation to contribute stability to any routine. By understanding each routine in only one context, and by defending that context as morally binding, the particular routines take on stability and a predictable character as a self-fulfilling prophecy.

This line of reasoning inverts the argument that the stability and predictability of relationships, their social factual character, is prior to the experience of commitment to them. Fortunately, these contending views can be tested empirically, at least in principle.

What are you really up to? (Garfinkel 1964). Special motives and unusual interpretations of ongoing activities that disturb established routines are interdicted and sanctioned by anger and resentment. When students experimentally adopted and acted upon the unusual premise that they were boarders, the responses of their families were vigorous and negative. In another procedure, Garfinkel was able to show that undue questioning of the meaning of others' actions was also forbidden. People are accountable to conduct themselves in accord with the usual understanding of events and relationships; people are accountable to accept that others are doing so without question.

Students were instructed to violate the typical presumption that others are trustworthy. Another person was to be treated as if a bit of quite ordinary behavior concealed an ulterior motive, a motive different from the usual meaning of the behavior. Perfectly obvious talk was to be treated as problematic, as grounds for further probing to uncover the hidden motive and avoid being misled.

These instructions were difficult to follow. Students experienced anxiety about being distrustful in this way and experienced fear of the consequences in anticipation of the exercise. The attempt to be distrustful proved difficult. Students found it difficult to construe that any deception was occurring and that the effort to not see things in the ordinary way was distracting. The expression of distrust produced anger and embarrassment for both parties. One woman demanded repeated assurances from a bus driver that the bus would indeed stop at the desired street. The bus driver eventually became angry and admonished her loudly enough for the other passengers to hear. In effect, he appealed to the others as witnesses to her unreasonableness. She was extremely embarrassed and reported knowing that the bus driver was right.

This demonstration obviously does not imply that distrust never occurs. In ordinary situations we can expect considerable disagreement over the appropriate limits of discretion. When does conduct become odd enough to justify questions about its motivation or negative responses to it? When is suspicion excessive? The questions are not rhetorical. Think about what principles might govern these practical judgments. We know that the issue is the disruption of routines. At some point, the continuation of odd behavior makes it difficult for others to continue in routine ways. Agnes's success in leaving others' routines undisturbed indicates that publicity is a factor. So does greater police tolerance of disrespect when no audience is present. Review the evidence you have studied thus far and determine which additional factors seem to influence the degree of reaction to oddness.

Rate the Candidate (Garfinkel 1964). The foregoing demonstrations, taken collectively, imply that the ability to understand events in such a way that one's subsequent conduct doesn't disturb others is a crucial social skill. One must be able to recognize the routine when one sees it, thus avoiding displays of unwarranted distrust; one must act as if one perceived the same environment as others did, thus not arousing their distrust. In fact, it proved possible to produce a breach by systematically contradicting a person in an emotionally significant situation.

The subjects of the study were premedical students. They were interviewed and given information about the qualities that medical schools prefer in candidates, advice on how to behave during admissions interviews, and so on. The students were then offered the opportunity to hear a tape recording of a medical school applicant. All were eager to hear the tape recording. The students were then asked to evaluate the candidate, based on the performance in the interview and were offered the results of the actual evaluation as a test of their own insight. The tape-recorded interview was a fake, of course, and the information was fabricated by the experimenter to contradict whatever the subject said about the interview.

In the taped interview, the applicant was boorish, spoke ungrammatically and colloquially, was evasive, contradicted the interviewer, bragged, bad-mouthed other schools and professions, and demanded to know how he had done in the interview. If the subject said the applicant was apparently from a lower-class family, a wealthy family background was provided in response. If the subject said the applicant could not work well with people, a history of successful fund raising with wealthy donors was mentioned. If the subject said the student was ignorant, a sparkling and eclectic academic career was cited.

The subjects responded to the initial contradictions by attempting to reconcile their interpretations with the facts. As contradictions mounted, subjects became confused and anxious and began to doubt their own ability to make adequate character assessments. The nature of this breach, produced by systematically denying social validation, is quite interesting. Faking a taped interview and fabricating information specifically to contradict another person are odd behaviors. But they are odd behaviors that are not necessarily recognized as such. Only three of twenty-eight subjects were not taken in by the deception. More important, the twenty-five students who believed that the contradictions were honest ones attributed the consistent pattern of disagreement to their own inadequacy in making character judgments. The competence of the experimenter was not called into question. The willingness to accept blame for disagreements is not necessarily found in other settings. The experimenter was in a position of considerable authority: a medical school admissions interviewer, in apparent possession of the real facts of the case, contesting the views of medical school applicants in his area of expertise.

If not generalizable, the willingness to accept blame is quite suggestive. We have already observed the infusion of moral accountability into discussions of fact. This connection is based upon, and protects, the assumption that there is a correct perception in any given situation and that disagreements are signs of error. The assumption, and its defense, are revealed by this experiment to be very strong. People will continue to assume that there is a single correct interpretation of events and to regard disagreements as signs of error even when they must conclude that they are in error, so severely in error, in fact, that they must question their own competence.

Bargaining (Garfinkel 1964). The breaches discussed thus far demonstrate that conduct is coordinated with reference to a variety of assumptions, protected from scrutiny by various defenses. But this knowledge has no radical implications for sociological theory in itself. All the results are to be expected, given the common sociological view that people orient themselves to really existing social norms. In ordinary sociological terms, these breaches show that, when someone violates rules that he or she is expected to follow, all involved exhibit anxiety, anger, and confusion, and social sanctions are applied. They do show strikingly, however, that the dynamics of role observance involves untested assumptions that act as self-fulfilling prophecies.

The credibility of the radical interpretation of these assumptions—the view that they demonstrate the inadequacy of formal logic as a model of everyday reasoning—is supported by an experiment in which students were assigned to bargain for the reduction of prices. Some students were assigned to one trial, others to a series of six. The students felt the greatest anxiety anticipating their first trials. Some refused to do the experiment. After a couple of trials, however, anxiety gave way to enjoyment of the exercise. The reaction of the shopkeepers was also important. They were not appalled or outraged. In fact, they engaged in the bargaining, and, in some instances, prices were lowered. Despite the anticipatory anxiety that the behavior would be out of line and despite the rarity of bargaining, no breach occurred. Everyone adapted to the situation.

The contrast between the severe anxiety with which the students anticipated bargaining and the ease with which it was actually conducted is instructive. In the other exercises, the disturbance of routine produced disorientation and confusion in the social situations involved. In effect, the assumptions that guided conduct in the routine ways were shown to be true—violating them caused trouble. But, here, a violation of those assumptions was achieved without making the environment senseless. Instead of confusion and social disorder, the result was simply that people bargained instead of passively accepting fixed prices. The assumptions that generated the severe anxiety about attempting to bargain were, in effect, proved false. The subjects were wrong to assume that attempting to bargain is a blameworthy act; they were wrong to assume that store personnel are not flexible enough to cope with bargaining; they were wrong to assume that bargaining would cause trouble.[4] Here the self-fulfilling character of assumptions, independent of their accuracy, is clearly highlighted.

[4] Perhaps they were wrong to assume that bargaining is uncommon. It is frequently done for certain large purchases, such as cars. Perhaps it occurs for lower-price items too.

Prior to the exercise, the students assumed that they could not bargain; they did not try; bargaining did not occur. It is such assumptions that structure everyday life, and they structure our lives whether they are accurate or inaccurate.

The flexibility of the subjects and the store personnel is also instructive. We have already seen that routine conduct can be modified by adopting an atypical, but still preformulated, plan of action. One can choose to act the boarder instead of the family member. But in such cases, it is only shown that the person can shift from one pre-programmed role to another. Now, it is clear that people are able to respond flexibly and extemporaneously to situations. People are able to successfully improvise a line of conduct and coordinate their activities with others without prior instruction or experience. They are able to act accountably without preformulated rules of conduct. The students were able to overcome their initial anxieties and begin bargaining in response to the practical motive provided by the class assignment; the store personnel were able to respond to the students without special motives. For them, it was all in a day's work. Garfinkel, in his most felicitous phrase, argues that this flexibility shows that people are not "dopes."

The bargaining exercise establishes several points about the structure of everyday life. First, assumptions protect established routines whether the assumptions are correct or not. The assumptions need not be shared either. Since the rules that people imagine to be operating are not tested, it is possible that different people assume different rules to be operating, different things to be going on. Successful interaction can be sustained, so long as the differences among the assumptions do not cause disturbances of the routine that are too severe for the task at hand. For example, sales personnel may assume that prices can be changed but that the posting of fixed prices implies that they can only lose in a bargain. Thus, they do not initiate bargaining (except for certain large purchases). Customers may think that the prices cannot be changed. Neither will initiate bargaining; both will abide by the posted price. In Agnes's efforts to be an accountable woman, we saw an extended discussion of how differing assumptions do not prevent accountable interaction.[5]

Second, we can still conceive that people learn to guide their conduct and interpret the conduct of others in terms of prelearned packages of rules called social rules. However, we cannot conceive that these rules must be clearly and precisely defined or that people must behave by following these rules in an uncreative way. Clerks can comprehend and interact with customers who violate important elements of the customer role by bargaining. Clerks and customers together can complete sales in nonroutine ways when, given a reason to do so,

---

[5]   Schelling (1979) discusses the formal implications of various distributions of intentions for the stabilization of routines of conduct in a population. In some cases, it is possible for routines to develop that are no one's preference but, nonetheless, are predictable consequences of people's seeking what they want.

the routine is abandoned. Once we acknowledge that people can improvise their conduct and still account for it, we can never be sure whether accounts of conduct were preformulated or were assembled on the spot. We can, of course, always formulate the nature of the routine to our own satisfaction, including routine remarks made by people as it progresses.

There is an exercise you can perform that should help to clarify this point. It will not cause a disturbance, and it should not make you unduly uncomfortable. The purpose of the exercise is to make a remark that convinces someone else that you have knowledge that you do not, in fact, have. From their responses, you will likely learn what you appear to have already known, and more. For example, while driving through a strange neighborhood with someone who is familiar with it, remark that the neighborhood has changed. This implies that you've been there before, but not since the changes occurred. The other person is very likely to look around and talk about the changes, filling you in on what he or she thought you knew and on recent events. In the same way, one can comment about prices in a store or restaurant, the variety of menu items, the decoration of a building or room, a friend's weight, the level of morale in a workplace, or the noise level of a cafeteria, bar, or doctor's waiting room. Once you've satisfied yourself that this can be done, think about how often it might have happened to you.[6] Think, too, about how you could ever know.

Third, the nature of "adequate for the purposes at hand" as a standard of accuracy is brought into focus. People assume that there is a final and obvious meaning to events and a proper way to act. They assume, further, that others share these definitions, and they assume that others also assume that they are shared. So long as activities proceed adequately for the purposes at hand, none of these matters is questioned. Even untoward conduct does not call these principles into question. Instead, it is assumed that someone is in error and that failure to satisfactorily resolve the difficulties is morally accountable. People feel anxiety; they anticipate the results of being found morally wanting when they plan to violate these assumptions. When assumptions are violated, others may respond with anger and hostility. The violator is inclined to uphold the principle of moral accountability by admitting error and feeling embarrassed by questioning his or her own competence or in other ways. Nonetheless, there are violations that are dreaded in anticipation but turn out in practice to be uneventful. The anticipatory anxiety, based perhaps on past experience, reduces testing of the boundaries of acceptable variation. The routine is upheld. The unquestioning acceptance of existing routines stabilizes them and limits questioning of what others really believe, what others will really accept, how nonroutine conduct will really be received. In the presence of these interlocking practices, our knowledge of these aspects of the social world remains adequate for all

[6]   This procedure is called Rose's gloss, after its creator, Edward Rose. It is discussed in more detail by Garfinkel and Sacks (1970).

practical purposes. We avoid trouble by upholding routines. We miss alternatives. We are practical. We follow the rule of thumb, "If it works, don't fix it."[7]

Trust in Tic-Tac-Toe and in Psychiatric Interviews

In one respect, at least, games are like social roles as sociologists usually conceive them. Both are governed by rules that define the options available to player-incumbents and influence the outcomes of their conduct. The same rules make the conduct of the player-incumbent explicable to others. Different games or roles have different rules. Knowledge of the role or game being played indicates what rules apply and what conduct is appropriate; from observed conduct we can estimate what rules are being followed and from that infer what role or game is being played. We have already seen that the accuracy of these estimates is protected from close evaluation by a variety of practices and can only be determined adequately for the purposes at hand.

The correspondence between roles and games makes it possible to gain insight into role behavior by studying relatively simple games. By violating the rules of a simple game in a fundamental way, one ought to be able to generate the perception that one is not playing the expected game, that one is not playing by the usual rules, or that one is not playing in an orderly way at all. From the response of others to such violations, we can learn something about the analogous violation of social rules. Hence, the tic-tac-toe study.

But games are not exactly like roles. In games, the stakes are generally lower (gambling excluded); the rules are generally more explicit; the natures of winning and losing are more clearly defined; the beginning and end are more distinctly marked; little self-esteem is sacrificed in terminating play; and the moves are more clearly communicated. These factors make it simpler to recognize that the rules are not being followed, less threatening to admit to that, and easier to terminate play. The study of the psychiatric interview shows that accountable interaction can continue despite severe misunderstandings about what is "really going on" so long as the appearance of following the expected rules is sustained. The knowledge gained from the study of tic-tac-toe games by disrupting them made it possible to create an artificial, but nondisruptive, environment in which the accounting process could still be readily observed.

The term *trust* has a slightly unusual meaning in this context. Trust is an attitude of confident prior belief that something will occur or that someone will behave as expected. It may be based on prior experience, but, in each particular case, when one trusts another, one is assuming how the other will act in the future. Usually, we use the word trust with respect to quite specific matters. We trust someone to return borrowed money. These specific beliefs support

---

[7]   This succinct formulation of the commonsense norm par excellence is indebted to Judith Rossner (1977).

specific practical decisions. The commonsense attitude, as we have seen, is a set of confidently held beliefs about the nature of the world and the proper way to conduct oneself in it. These beliefs are often quite global and abstract, but they still enter crucially into practical decision making. It is trust as a global attitude with which we are concerned—not trust in particular, well-defined matters. In effect, to trust is to take the commonsense attitude. This is not a far-fetched extension of the term trust, since each particular trusting belief is supported and sustained by the global assumptions of the commonsense attitude and tested only by the practical standards it imposes.

In the tic-tac-toe study (Garfinkel 1963), sixty-seven students were used as experimenters. Each played tic-tac-toe with three or more subjects of various ages and with whom they had various relationships. The subjects were invited to move first. After they placed their initial mark, the experimenter erased it, moved it to another cell, and placed his or her own mark. The experimenter acted as nonchalant as possible while doing this. The experimenter then recorded the responses of the subjects.

The interpretations of the experimenter's odd conduct fell into three categories. Some subjects felt that the experimenter was trying a new game or was playing tic-tac-toe in a new way. They abandoned tic-tac-toe as a point of reference and adopted a new principle for ordering the situation—a new, unknown game was being played. This interpretation was associated with little emotional disturbance. Some subjects attempted to retain tic-tac-toe as a point of reference. They felt that the experimenter was cheating or ruining the game. This response was associated with the most emotional disturbance. These subjects responded similarly to family members (who also did not abandon their normal frames of reference) when confronted with a member acting as a boarder. Some subjects decided that tic-tac-toe was not being played but did not reach any conclusion concerning what was actually going on. Was this a sexual pass? Was the experimenter ridiculing the subject? This reaction was associated with intermediate levels of emotional reaction.

We can hazard these interpretations of the results. The more one is committed to the continuation of existing routines (game rules, for example), the more emotionally one will respond to their disturbance. The more consequential the alteration of the existing routine appears, the more emotionally one will react to it. For example, those who thought they were encountering a new variation of tic-tac-toe were calm relative to those who thought they were being ridiculed. Whether it is a matter of willingness or facility, the ability to redefine situations rather than attempting to treat surprises as violations of an existing arrangement seems to mitigate the emotional impact of confusion and surprises. Both those who settled on the idea that a new game was being played and those who knew something odd was afoot, something that was not tic-tac-toe, but did not reach an understanding of what was happening, responded with less emotion than did those who saw events as a violation of the existing rules.

We can draw a methodological lesson from these reactions to the tic-tac-toe variations. There are some criteria that, if met, will occasion attempts to redefine ongoing events without generating a breach or the emotional responses that go with it. That is, we can devise situations in which reasoning occurs and accounting is easily observed as data without dramatically disturbing the peace of everyday life. The criteria are these: We must establish a situation that is noticeably strange for situations of its type but that appears, at the same time, to be accountable as an acceptable variation of such situations. In the tic-tac-toe experiment, one group responded in that way. The subjects knew that the game being played was strange for tic-tac-toe, but they could still perceive it as a variation of tic-tac-toe or, at least, as an accountably friendly game.

The psychiatric interview study was designed to achieve this effect. A highly unusual therapy situation was fabricated, but most subjects continued to accept it as accountable therapy. As the subjects discussed their problems and the therapy technique, accounting practices were conveniently exhibited without a breach.

The psychiatric interview study employed ten volunteer subjects, all undergraduate students. They were told that the experiment was intended to explore new psychiatric techniques. Each subject was asked to discuss the background to a serious problem with an experimenter. The experimenter was falsely identified as a counselor in training. The subjects were then to ask the counselor a series of questions about the problem that could be answered "yes" or "no." The experimenter heard the questions and gave the answers from an adjoining room by using an intercom system. The subjects described their problems aloud, asked their questions, and after receiving a yes or no answer disconnected their link to the experimenter so that they could not be heard. During this time, the subjects tape-recorded their comments about the exchange (These comments were to be used, so the subjects were told, to evaluate the procedure of separating counselors and clients and forcing the clients to think their problems through until direct, simple questions could be posed.) After the entire series of questions, overall comments about the procedure were recorded and the subjects were interviewed. The series of yes and no answers was the same for all subjects. It was predetermined by consulting a table of random numbers. The answers had nothing to do with the questions, although they may still, by happenstance, have been fine advice. Whew!

Apparently, the subjects were successfully deceived. They asked questions, ruminated about the answers aloud, and gave evaluations of the therapy procedure that doubted its effectiveness but not its reality. The prior determination of the yes/no series produced occasional contradictions in the advice. One student was sequentially told that he could and could not improve his study habits and could and could not get a degree. The subject made no comment about the contradictions. Perhaps he did not notice; perhaps he thought that the intervening exchange had changed the counselor's mind. No question was raised over the existence of the counselor or the motivation of answers by questions.

The subjects responded to the answers in posing subsequent questions. No subject had a preselected series of questions. The subjects assumed that the experimenter's answers were similarly responsive. For example, one subject discussed family problems that he expected to arise from his relationship with a woman of another faith. He was told not to ask her to change her religion. He reflected aloud about this advice until arriving at his next question, which concerned another way to deal with the religious differences.

Despite the peculiar limitation that the counselor would say only yes or no, the subjects responded as if they were in an accountable conversation. They took it upon themselves to fill in the reasoning behind the yes or no and to determine what it meant when its implications were more fully developed. We can see here that the indexical particulars in a conversation can be quite limited —yes and no answers, stripped of nonverbal supplementary cues—and still provide adequate information for the rest to be filled in by consulting the already known appropriate contextual information.[8] As in the other exercises, subjects referred consistently to the one and proper context for the case at hand. To say that they were deceived is to say that they never questioned the relevance of that correct context or tried to reinterpret the answers using another body of contextual information. Steadfastly, the subjects interpreted the yes/no sequence as originating in the consideration of an actual therapist of their actual problems during an actual therapy session. Even in this highly unusual conversation, subjects were not led to question what the counselor was "really up to."

Most important, the subjects searched for an underlying pattern in the yes/no sequence. This search had several aspects. First, the subjects filled in considerable background information about what each yes or no meant and why the counselor answered as he or she did. Told not to continue dating a woman of another faith, the subject speculated that the counselor could foresee greater family tension over his relationship than existed at the time. That is, yes and no were treated as indexical remarks in two senses. They were seen as answers to particular questions. They were also seen as capable of satisfactory clarification by being put into juxtaposition with appropriate additional knowledge. What the yes or no was (an answer) and what it meant were both understood by drawing on other things the subject knew.

Second, the subjects' own questions were indexical in the same ways. The subjects formulated each successive question in the course of speculating about the meaning of the counselors' answers. Each new question was reasonable by virtue of its connection to the previous series of questions and answers. Each question reflected the subject's understanding of that sequence. Each new question acted as a test, for the subject, of how well previous answers had been

---

[8]   Haire (1968) clearly establishes that people are capable of making judgments when the available information is extremely limited. In his experiment, subjects were able to make character judgments by bringing background knowledge to bear on a single shopping list.

understood, as well as a stimulus for further advice. Each new answer clarified what came before. The counselor was understood to mean more than he or she said. An accountable line of reasoning was assumed to underlie each yes or no answer. Subjects were willing to wait for this meaning to become clear and acted in a manner that was calculated to clarify it.

Third, subjects were able to make accountable sense of the incomplete and occasionally contradictory answers. In part, the sketchiness of the answers given by the therapists was repaired by the subjects' activities. They filled in reasonable interpretations of what the counselor meant and designed their questions to seek supplementary information necessary to understand the entire sequence better. Remaining vagueness was attributed to the inadequacies of the therapy procedure. That is, the subjects regarded incompleteness in the perceived pattern of advice as a structurally induced error and persevered in the format until their comprehension was adequate for the situation at hand. Adequacy reflects both the amount of information one needs and the availability of the information in the current circumstances.

Contradictory answers, which occurred occasionally, posed a special problem for interpretation. The occasional contradictions, however, did not lead the subjects to question the counselor's competence or the nature of the counselor's involvement in the session. I have already mentioned one instance of contradiction. A student was told at one point in the interview that he could improve his study habits and graduate. Later in the interview, in response to successive questions he was told he could not improve his habits sufficiently, could not expect to graduate, and should quit school. This subject did not make notice of the contradiction between the earlier and later answers. Simply not noticing contradictions is one manner in which reasonable patterns can be sustained.

In another case a subject asked whether he should continue dating a woman of another faith despite family misgivings. The answer was no. The answer surprised the subject who speculated that an objective observer might be able to foresee more severe family problems that he was oblivious to. The subject then asked whether he should continue discussions with his father about the situation. The answer was yes. The subject then asked whether he should continue to date the woman if his father reacted in a particular way during the discussion. The answer was yes. Apparently, the unqualified advice to stop dating the woman was not understood as unqualified. Rather, the subject understood that exceptions might be possible. In fact, he appears to have been actively seeking such exceptions. Logically, the unqualified advice not to date the woman and the later advice to date her under specific circumstances are contradictory. However, one manner of handling contradictions is to understand that apparently general, unqualified rules and statements admit to qualifications and exceptions. These are assumed to be present even if they have not been spelled out. Thus, the counselor is not incompetent for giving a qualified yes after an unqualified no and the yes and no are not understood to be contradictory. This way of understanding rules to have unstated exceptions and qualifications is a very important formal characteristic of everyday understandings. It allows logical contradictions to be accommodated in a single interpretation of events, and it allows rule violations and contradictions to be treated as exceptions to still valid rules. This eliminates the need to thoroughly question or reformulate the rule.

Some subjects became suspicious because the answers did not seem sensible or were blatantly contradictory. But it was difficult to sustain this doubt. Even when they voiced suspicion, subjects continued to see the sense of answers in the therapeutic frame. This parallels other findings that an attitude of distrust is hard to sustain and act upon.

In general, the subjects constructed accountable patterns through the use of the documentary method of interpretation. The known patterns gave sense to the particular answers which, in turn, were the available data that normal events, fitting the known pattern, were occurring. The known patterns function as powerful assumptions that predispose us to interpret events as continuing to fit the pattern. Trust in the continued relevance of these patterns supports patience and tolerance of considerable difficulty in communication while we attempt to clarify new information. In this study, it is clear that the general cultural background knowledge of the therapist is respected as a context for interpretation. Sometimes, the absence of specific information about the particular circumstances was acknowledged as a cause of incongruous answers. But sometimes this same absence of knowledge was acknowledged as providing a more objective perspective. Knowledge of the typical run of events is accountable expertise for discussing particular cases. It has advantages and disadvantages relative to specific knowledge of the case at hand.

What to Make of the Breaches, etc.

The breaches and other manipulative research designs have been replaced, for the most part, by direct observation and interviewing techniques. As sources of data, the breaches were a response to a peculiar set of circumstances. The philosophical writings of Schutz and Mannheim's methodological discussions suggested roughly what the commonsense attitude was and how everyday reasoning was done. They pointed to these topics as crucial for the understanding of social life. But the commonsense attitude, as we have seen, is difficult to observe. It is protected from close scrutiny by a variety of practices and by a formal structure that reduces awareness of contradiction and alternative ways of acting and thinking. Thus, it was necessary to intentionally disrupt the commonsense attitude and to observe the accounting activities by which it was reestablished.

Beginning with activities observed during a period of disruption is not at all unlike the medical practice of beginning medical students' surgical experience on cadavers. The organs are not working quite as they did in a routinely operating organism, nor do they look or feel quite the same. Still, the similarities are sufficient so that working on a cadaver is a great help in finding one's way around the interior of a living person with a knife, through x-ray pictures, or by feel. The study of the workings of the normal brain by analyzing the results of known brain damage is another similar practice. Brain damage is even inflicted on subjects for the purposes of study, at least on infrahuman subjects.

As the studies progressed, it became possible to create experimental environments that provided convenient data without breaching the commonsense attitude. Still later, as knowledge of what accounting practices look like and knowledge of their formal structure improved, it became possible to observe their occurrence fruitfully in undisturbed situations. The studies discussed in Chapter 1 are examples. Theoretically, any situation is a suitable one for study. But, as a practical matter, accounting activities are more easily observed in some situations than in others. Notice that all the studies in Chapter 1 involved the characterization of problem behavior in the context of bureaucratic categories and rules. Apparently, fitting behavior into preset bureaucratic categories is enough of a problem that accounting practices become conveniently observable.

A second characteristic of the breaches and other exercises is that they were useful as pedagogical devices. You may have noticed, as I described the various studies, that the usual practice was to assign undergraduate students to participate in them. The students, studying ethnomethodology in class, were provided with a special motive to make the commonsense attitude observable to them as an object of study. In class and in reading assignments, I imagine, the intellectual concerns of ethnomethodology were expounded. Participation in the breaches provided experiential knowledge in two important dimensions. First, the students experienced the confusion, resentment, anger, and so on, that accompany the failure of routine efforts to sustain the sense of an ordered world. Second, with the intellectual guidance provided in class, some of the students were, perhaps, able to experience the commonsense attitude—to see it as an object. During periods of disruption, guided by intellectual background knowledge, the commonsense attitude may have become perceptible; students may have been able to see how it operated to produce and sustain the experience of other objects and sustain the characteristic formal structure of events.

There is a difference between experiential and intellectual knowledge, to be sure. Still, I have not recommended the breaches as exercises. Nor am I about to do so. There is a value in experiencing a breach of the commonsense attitude as such and becoming aware of what such breaches reveal. But there is an accompanying cost in confusion and social disruption. I am a little squeamish about advising people to disrupt their lives, even in small ways, when I cannot equally well instruct them in the procedures for reassembling them. The effects of the disruptions are not necessarily trivial. Recall that in several of the breaching exercises anger and resentment were produced and were not removed by apologies. There is a real danger that, once breached, relationships may not be fully restorable. That observation and a fable to which it serves as a moral have survived for over two thousand years.[9] Folk wisdom of such duration should not be casually disregarded.

Besides, it is not necessary to manufacture breaches. Unfortunately they occur with great regularity. Breaches occur whenever our expectations are disappointed in a way that frustrates our efforts to coordinate activities with others on a basis that seems to include shared understandings. This situation can occur whenever intimate relationships disintegrate. Friends fall out; married couples divorce; children rebel against their parents; people lose their jobs and cannot find new ones. Generally, any of these unhappy events produces more confusion and disorientation than pretending to be a boarder in one's home for fifteen minutes. Breaches are not always the result of this confusion, but they are not uncommon. I do advise you to attend to these confusing periods as possible sites of naturally occurring breaches. The change in perspective may help you through the situation. It may give you added insight in any advice you offer. In any event, you can observe how people reason, explain themselves, and reestablish order or what happens when they are unable to do so.

Considered as a group of demonstrations, the breaches and other exercises that I have described are redundant. Each is not so much an advance to a new topic as a slightly different approach to the common task: exposing and formulating the attitude of everyday life. Together, they do not form a cumulative literature with each study adding discrete information to our body of knowledge. Instead, they constitute a set of variations on a theme. In addition, the findings are not as distinct and concise as those of most research. Garfinkel, in fact, cautions that many of his observations are not "findings" and that the studies are not actually experimental. He refers to his exercises and demonstrations as "aids to a sluggish imagination" (1967, p. 38).

This designation bears some explanation. Garfinkel was influenced greatly by the work of the phenomenological philosophers. The phenomenologists developed a method of investigation called *free fantasy variation*. The method was designed to abstract the core, or essential elements, of particular kinds of experiences so that those experiences could be analyzed and discussed precisely.

Suppose that one wanted to be precise in his or her analysis of the experience of an apple. Suppose that one wanted to know what was indispensable to that experience—what was common to any experience of an apple. To know

---

[9]   Daly (1961) includes this fable under the title "The snake that brought wealth." The moral is worded, "Once a friendship has been seriously damaged, it can hardly ever be entirely restored." Aesop's fables and other stories with formulated moral lessons are excellent resources for studying commonsense reasoning. Those, like Aesop's, that have stood the test of time can be understood to display superlative reasoning not closely bound to one time and place.

this, one would have to distinguish between the central or essential features common to experiences of apples and incidental experiences that sometimes are, and sometimes are not, part of that experience. Actual apples do not enter this procedure, nor are we discussing apples. We are discussing the experience of apples. We have a word—apple—and an experience to which that word refers. We are trying to be precise; we are trying to state precisely what a person has in mind when he or she describes what he or she has in mind as an apple.[10]

First, imagine an apple. Really conjure up an image. If it will help, look at an apple, but the presence of the apple is irrelevant to the procedure. We are concerned here with the sort of image that deserves the name "apple," not the sort of fruit that does. Now, pursuing clarity and precision, think about what makes that image or experience an image of an apple instead of an image of something else. Does changing the color matter? Will it still be an apple-image if we change its color? Is color essential to the experience of an apple? To find out, vary the color of the image. Make it red, yellow, green, brown, black, blue, white, magenta. Make it mauve, vermilion, salmon, chartreuse. But don't change anything else about the image. If a change in color changes the apple to something else, then that change establishes one of the essential boundaries of what an experience must be to be an apple experience. In this way you will discover, I believe, that apples can be many colors but not any color. Now alter the shape of the apple in your mind. Now alter the taste of the apple. Now alter the edibility of the apple. Proceed to identify every element of your experience of an apple; identify the variable of which it is a value (e.g., if your image is red, identify red as a value of the variable color). Then systematically explore what values of the variable can be substituted for your original one without transforming the entire experience from an experience of one kind (an apple) into an experience of another kind.

By this procedure, we could specify a precise definition of the term "apple." In everyday use, when applied to real fruits, the term apple will still be a loose or indexical one. However, we will have established a precisely defined category that will allow us to talk logically about our experiences of apples if not about apples.

Garfinkel's exercises and demonstrations are a clever adaptation of this procedure to the task of understanding the social world. What is essential, and what is peripheral, to our experience of the social world and our experience that is orderly and real? To find out, we vary the features of various situations to see what will transform them into experiences of another kind. The act of transformation reveals the formal structure of the experience. But the attitude of everyday life defends itself against close examination. It even defends itself

---

[10]   The frequently used technical term "intended object" can be adequately understood to refer to "the object as it appears in the mind." Intended purpose, intended course of action, intended meaning, and so on, all conform to that usage.

specifically against varying the context of interpretation. So, instead of trying to overcome these defenses unaided, actual situations are manipulated. The unusual circumstances aid us in overcoming the defenses of the commonsense attitude. They aid us in imagining alternatives and becoming aware of our experiences and our ways of experiencing in a new way.

There is also a parallel in the breaches and other demonstrations to the firm distinction between the apple, or any object, and its image. We have seen that untested assumptions about the world structure our everyday lives, even when the assumptions prove untrue when tested. In the study of practical reasoning, ethnomethodologists are interested in discovering people's assumptions, but they are relatively uninterested in whether those assumptions are true. What actors believe and how they think must be specified in the study of practical reasoning. Action is based on these assumptions and calculations. But, since the assumptions structure life regardless of their truth and since they tend to be self-fulfilling as well, it is not always necessary to distinguish between accurate and inaccurate assumptions to understand practical reasoning and everyday life. Remember the peace-keeping activities of the skid-row police. Their rounds and treatment of the inhabitants of skid row are ordered by their beliefs about the types of persons who live on skid row. Whether those beliefs are true or not is a factual question that is largely irrelevant to understanding the reasoning behind police practices.

The manipulation of social situations is not essential to Garfinkel's approach but, rather, serves as a convenient opening wedge. The study of Agnes, for example, exploits a naturally occurring provocative situation. Agnes was what she was without experimental help. Becoming aware of her unusual situation produces the shock necessary to reflect upon our experience of gender and sex roles without experimental manipulation. Agnes is a variation of our experience that we might have difficulty producing without the impetus provided by her empirical presence. Without an occasional transsexual to remind us that nature has an extremely unsluggish imagination for producing variety, could we as easily transcend the typical and consider the implications of the variation "woman with a penis"?

SUGGESTED READINGS

Breaches and other quasi-experimental manipulations are not frequently used by ethnomethodologists any longer. Nonetheless, they are important to understanding the development of thought in the specialty. In addition to Garfinkel's demonstrations (1963; 1964; 1967), which I have discussed, McHugh's (1968) is an excellent example of this type of research. It is based on McHugh's doctoral dissertation, and its discussions of methodology and connections to theoretical issues in sociology are more explicit than are Garfinkel's shorter reports.

4

Further Specification of the Commonsense Attitude: Cross-Purposes in Natural Settings

STUDIES IN UNDISTURBED SETTINGS

In natural settings, undisturbed by efforts to breach the natural attitude, people seldom notice or talk about sense-making activities. But the study that successfully exploited a sham psychiatric interview demonstrates that sense-making activities are revealed when people talk about their practical problems. The form of accountable arguments can be inferred by examining the arguments that people respect enough to offer on their own behalves and to let pass when they are offered by others. Talk is not essential to the study of practical reason, which occurs whether people talk aloud or not. However, talk, especially talk about problems, provides the most convenient data for study.

As a rule, people talk most when there are others around to talk to, especially when their activities must be coordinated. Whatever other problems people discuss, the coordination of their activities provides additional purposes. As a result, ethnomethodological studies are almost invariably concerned with the reconciliation of conflicting interests or cross-purposes. Even where people's priorities are clear and consensual, the need to coordinate their activities when problems arise with the routine way of acting imposes additional purposes that must be served while addressing other problems. In effect, then, the naturalistic ethnomethodological studies are focused upon the reasoning that becomes explicit when problems arise due to conflicting interests or cross-purposes. The theoretical import of the reasoning is broader, but the empirical content has been narrowly defined as a response to the practical considerations of gathering data.

Good Reasons for Bad Clinic Records

A naturally occurring breach was instrumental in Garfinkel's study of bureaucratic record-keeping procedures in a clinic (1967). Garfinkel and Bittner were attempting to conduct a statistical study of the process through which applicants were selected for outpatient treatment at a psychiatric clinic. Clinic records were to be the source of data—especially the intake application form and the contents of the case folders. Together, these items should have included the relevant demographic information about the patient and the medical commentary on his or her case. A special clinic career form was designed on which every transaction between patients and the clinic was to be recorded. Thus, they hoped to obtain records of the demographic characteristics of the patients, initial medical evaluation of them, and a record and evaluation of each contact between the patient and the clinic staff. From these data, they could construct the typical career lines of the patients. They could establish what was involved in the original decision to accept the patient, trace the ways in which different kinds of patients were handled in the clinic, and establish the grounds for termination of treatment.

The breach, a mild and convenient one, was precipitated by the persistent failure of the files to include the desired information despite the presence of forms on which the staff were instructed to record it. The clinic's own official forms were also filled out incompletely. The persistent trouble in acquiring data led to reflection on how the files were kept. That is, how did the clinic staff account for their patient contacts? The patients' files were compiled as part of the routine operation of the clinic. To understand the files, including their characteristic incompleteness, one must study their compilation as an organizational activity among other organizational activities of the clinic. Good, practical reasons were found for the persistent refusal of staff to provide "good" records. Those reasons were the routine practical problems for which the incomplete record-keeping was a practical solution. In addition, the contents of the files proved difficult to interpret, except by reference to knowledge about the routine operation of the clinic. The files were the product of bureaucratic routines of perception. While specific details may vary from setting to setting, the difficulties in acquiring "good" records are common in bureaucratic settings, and for similar reasons.

Practical concerns of the clinic staff were at the heart of the persistent problem of incomplete files. The clinic staff had established routines for recording information, keeping track of patients, and making sense of events in the clinic. These standardized ways of keeping and interpreting records were linked to the staff's own routine needs for information. Some kinds of information were regularly needed for both medical and bureaucratic activities. Other information, although requested on forms, was not regularly needed and was recorded only erratically. The incomplete reporting did not improve, despite the persuasive efforts of the research team and the clinic administration.

Among the information needed for the purposes of research were items not needed by the staff. This conflict of interests resulted in files that were adequate for the operation of the clinic but inadequate for the research project. There was no taint of incompetence. There were simply two different uses to be made of the files. The researchers intended to get staff cooperation in obtaining data. But they were requesting that the clinic staff consistently and carefully record data that were useless to them. That is, the researchers wanted the clinic staff to act impractically, and in this they did not succeed. The files remained persistently incomplete because the clinic staff remained persistently practical.

The record-keeping of the staff disappointed the needs of the researchers. This kind of disappointment will occur, in a form appropriate to the circumstances, whenever people with different practical purposes depend upon one another as collaborators. And, since people work together even while apart, disappointment of this type will occur whenever people pursue their diverse practical goals. This disappointment is a normal, natural trouble; it is a natural state of affairs.[1]

I do not mean to imply that the intended sociological research would not have been useful to the clinic and to some of its staff. The difficulty, as I have described it so far, was that those members of the staff who were being asked to record the information had no practical interest in doing so. The information about patient careers would have been interesting primarily for administrative purposes. The potential use of the information within the clinic, in ways that could not be anticipated and in ways that could not be controlled, provided the medical staff with a reason to resist recording it. Here, then, is a second good reason for bad clinic records. Not only was the medical staff uninterested in the data, but the data were interesting to others in a potentially threatening way.

Among the uses to which records may be put is that of helping to decide whether or not the clinic staff performed their duties competently. The clinic staff was accountable for its treatment of clients. They were subject to various internal and external sanctions that enforced that accountability.[2] Whatever was contained in clinic records served as an official account of activities in the clinic. These accounts were prepared with concerned awareness that they would ultimately be used as a basis for evaluation. Information that was requested, but did not appear to be relevant to the staff's understanding of its duties, was problematic. This was especially so when the relevance of the information was not clear. Consider the situation from the perspective of the medical staff. They had been working and reporting their work in a standardized manner. A research team, with the support of the clinic administration, expressed interest in information about how decisions were made in the clinic. This information had no utility in their own duties, but it could be used to evaluate their performance by new and unknown standards. Staff members did not know what would be made of the new information or, through it, of them. They were wary of reporting it since reporting it would possibly be a confession of unknown and previously unnoticed inadequacies.

In this discussion, I have stressed that the clinic files were chronically incomplete but that, although they were inadequate for research purposes, they were adequate for use by the clinic staff. Now I should like to indicate how the two approaches to the files differed. Members of the clinic's medical staff had considerable background knowledge about the routine operation of the clinic based on their participation in its activities. This background knowledge served as context for the specific entries in the files. The files were indexical.

---

[1]   See Toulmin (1961) for a discussion of the term "natural state of affairs." See W. Handel (1979) for an argument that this kind of disappointment is ubiquitous, negotiable, and structurally based.

[2]   Schelling (1960) argues that sanctions are a necessary condition for accountability. A person may promise or contract to perform in a certain way, but, without enforceable sanctions, a person cannot be held accountable to do so.

They could only be understood in the context of assumed background information. Each file contained the information necessary to understand the case if one already knew about the routine operations of the clinic. In making entries, the medical staff assumed that this background knowledge was available to the reader. In interpreting entries, background knowledge was employed to fill in the complete meaning of the files.

The researchers were unable to read meaning into the files in the same way. In the first place, they were not members of the clinic staff. They lacked the necessary background information and access to informal sources of information about particular cases and about the operation of the clinic. But, even if the researchers had developed adequate background knowledge to interpret the files, they could not accountably do it. In the practical task of doing research, the method of data collection is as important as the accuracy of the data. In fact, the collection of data by scientifically sound procedures, the use of sound methodology, is the only acceptable guarantee of accuracy. Unlike the staff, the researchers were not able to fill in unrecorded information because they knew from experience how things were always done in the clinic. Nor could the researchers utilize informal sources to verify their interpretations. The researchers required explicitly recorded data that they were bound to read as literally as possible.

We have already seen several examples of how practical interests influence the relevance of information. Now we can also see that practical interests influence the evaluation of sources of information and acceptability of forms of reasoning. Differing standards of credibility allow public channels of information to carry a variety of messages, each of which is recognizable to only a fraction of those who have access to the channels.[3] In this case, information was made readily available to medical staff members in the files, while researchers with access to the files were unable to recover the information. "Knowing the ropes" includes knowing how to gather information in an appropriate way as well as developing the necessary background knowledge that staff members are held accountable to draw upon.

Making Sense of Goofing Off

The salaries of industrial workers are commonly based on either the amount of time spent on the job, usually computed at an hourly rate, or the amount of work done, usually computed at a piecework rate. Hourly pay motivates the worker to punch in and out at appropriate times, but further efforts may be needed to motivate performance while the worker is on the job. Piecework compensation is an attempt to provide incentives for diligent work

---

[3]   Goffman (1959) discusses the intentional development of codes based on recognition of this principle. Sales personnel, for example, develop signs for communicating about customers in their presence.

by basing payment on the amount of work actually completed. But observations of piecework shops have consistently revealed considerable loafing. Workers complete work at a slower pace than they could easily manage. Some actually stop for extended periods of time to nap, play cards, or socialize. These activities, it seems, would lower the workers' pay. So why are they done?

During the late 1930s and 1940s, industrial sociologists, taking a dim view of laborers' intelligence and rationality, came to this conclusion: Workers simply cannot understand the complex economic logic employed by management or the complex economic incentives that are offered. This incapacity is aggravated by frequent changes due to technological innovation. Workers become frustrated because they cannot understand their circumstances. As a result, they develop a "lower" social code which includes restriction of output. Intellectual incapacity and emotion combine to produce and support economically irrational group norms.

This was the sociologists' eye view of the matter, but a view achieved by studying industry at the sufferance of management. Permission to study the setting came from management, and management provided access to records and informants. The problem is interesting to management personnel because they want to increase production, to which end they require the cooperation of labor. But keep in mind that increased production is a means to the end of profit, not an unquestioned end in itself. This fact will make the workers' understanding of the situation seem sensible, too.

Roy (1952) did his study while working as a radial drill operator in a machine shop. He recorded his own production openly in the shop and made a daily record of shop activities, including his feelings and his conversations with others, at the end of each workday. He did not reveal his research interests to anyone in the shop. He had only the information available to ordinary workers. The result is a sociological study from the workers' perspective, supplemented only by the aid to memory provided by keeping a diary. The study is interesting because it takes that unusual point of view (unusual for an academic study) and because the conflicting interpretations of events are held by participants in the shop rather than by the participants and marginally involved researchers. This provides a good view of how conflicting interpretations are accommodated by the regular participants in a social setting.

To Roy, the production- and wage-reducing activities appeared to be of two distinct types: goldbricking and quota restriction. Quota restriction refers to the practice of slowing the pace of work, or stopping completely, when production reaches an informally set maximum level. Goldbricking refers to slowing the pace of work, or stopping completely, when production falls to an informally set minimum level despite normal efforts. Both practices appear to reduce the workers' income. But both practices are justified by complex economic reasoning, although not the line of reasoning proposed by management.

Pieceworkers in Roy's shop were guaranteed a minimum hourly wage. This

wage was paid while the workers were retooling their machines and were, therefore, temporarily not producing and while the workers were working on jobs
that went slowly and brought the piecework earnings below the guaranteed
minimum. There was tension, of course, in establishing the piecework rate.
Management tended to want the price per piece set lower than labor. When the
price of a new item was being set, workers slowed down their production considerably to give the impression that the job was difficult. Workers believed,
too, that, if they worked too fast on an existing job, management would react
to their increased wages by reducing the price per piece.

On easy jobs, the workers reduced their efforts so that their wages, based
on piecework rates, would not exceed an hourly level that workers thought
would be acceptable to management. If their piecework production resulted in
an unacceptably high rate of pay, they would slow down or stop so that their
average production over the eight-hour work period would be acceptable. The
workers sustained an informal norm concerning management's boundaries of
acceptable wages. They taught the norms to new workers and oriented their
production to it. This was a restriction. On difficult jobs, workers felt that their
best efforts were not justified by the difference between the guaranteed hourly
wage and the results of sustained effort at the piecework rate. They reduced
their level of effort, lost some money, and accepted the hourly wage. Once a job
got a bad reputation, workers did not even try to make a good wage. If they
could not avoid the job, they assumed that they could not make an acceptable
wage and, hence, worked slowly. This was goldbricking.

Labor and management, each pursuing its own interests, behaved in ways
that were sensible to all involved. However, the two groups made strikingly
different sense of events in the shop. The workers, assuming that management
would set piecework rates artificially low, purposely attempted to mislead
management when new jobs were being timed. This created jobs that were overpriced by management's standards. To avoid detection on easy jobs, workers
contrived to work slowly so that the job would not be repriced. Working slowly
prevented real tests of labor's assumptions about how management would
respond. It also provided management with evidence of bad faith by workers and
of workers' failure to respond to economic incentives. The evidence of bad faith
justified management's alertness for overpriced jobs, occasional retiming, and
distrust of slow work while new jobs were being timed. All these responses
justified labor's beliefs that management would respond to excessive wages by
retiming and repricing existing jobs. The purposeful slowdown on easy jobs
tended to reduce the credibility of complaints about hard ones. Management
resisted repricing them, although repricing would have increased production.
Management's resistance to repricing hard jobs supported labor's assumption
that management could not be trusted to honor honest efforts to increase production. Periodic deviation from informal norms that lead to the retiming of
easy jobs provided labor with proof that a decent wage could only be made by

quota restriction and misleading management. At the same time, these discoveries of intentional slowdowns provided management with proof that labor was uncooperative and failed to respond rationally to economic incentives.

The assumptions of each group about itself and others led to routines of behavior that concealed alternatives from it. Each group had characteristic interests which led to characteristic routines of perception and to characteristic versions of what was going on. Each group understood events in the shop only by reference to its own underlying pattern of prior understandings. And each group, with its different interests, perceived a different pattern. The two understandings coexisted without dramatic discomfort or remedy. Events in the shop made sense to both groups, but they did not make the same sense to both groups. Apparently, it is not necessary for the continuation of organized social life that different people and groups share definitions of what is going on. Much is left unsaid, to be filled in from background knowledge. So long as events are sensible within the various frameworks imposed on them, the various participants understand events and are able to sustain routinized activities.[4]

Two complementary aspects of communication with indexical expressions are revealed in this. First, as we have already observed, events can be interpreted in various ways without interrupting routine patterns of behavior. Leaving things unsaid, then, supports chronic, but unnoticed, misunderstandings between people with different background knowledge. Second, the use of indexical expressions prevents the misunderstandings from becoming noticed. Leaving things unsaid makes it possible for the different interpretations to be held without being noticed. If people pursued the meaning of the indexical utterances more diligently aloud, and in the wrong company, the differences in interpretation would become clear to participants, as it has to researchers. Leaving things unsaid, while assuming that they have been understood, then, is another way in which the commonsense attitude is protected from scrutiny. This protective procedure involves cooperative efforts from the various participants. It is a communication procedure, expressed in overt conduct, not one confined to an individual's inferences. Perhaps the sense that this procedure of routine conduct has been violated helps to generate the anger and embarrassment that occur when people are pressed to explain matters too fully or are distrusted too openly.

Making a Queue Move Smoothly— Maintaining a Simple Routine

Conflicts among practical interests are not restricted to interpersonal differences. Often, one person has multiple practical interests or tasks to be completed. Often, to work on one task is to neglect another or, worse yet, to

---

[4]   Periodically, these routine arrangements break down. In the reckoning of both groups, labor and management, previously unmentioned assumptions are explicated. Basic differences are revealed and intergroup relationships disintegrate. These episodes are accompanied by considerable tension and reactions as extreme, sometimes, as strikes. See Roy (1954) and Gouldner (1954).

undermine its completion. It is difficult to indulge a sweet tooth and maintain a weight reduction diet at the same time. In such situations, a person's routines or habits will interrupt one another, necessitating corrective efforts and making accounting activities visible. A study by Don Zimmerman (1970) illustrates one such conflict in a simple bureaucratic task—assigning waiting clients to caseworkers in a public assistance organization. The extreme simplicity of the task is important. Conflicts of this kind are not confined to complex situations. Even the simplest routines need attention and repair. The appearance of accounting activities in very simple situations heightens the credibility of the claim that these activities are the essence of social life. As the practical troubles in which these activities can be convincingly demonstrated become increasingly trivial, the notion that they continue unnoticed, perhaps undemonstrably, when there is no trouble at all, is strengthened.

When clients arrive at the public assistance agency, their first contact was with a receptionist. The receptionist screened the clients, determining what type of assistance each was an applicant for. The receptionist collected relevant data from the clients—name, age, residence, and so on—to begin or update the files and then assigned the applicants to an intake worker. The assignment to an intake worker was on a first-come, first-served basis. Part of the receptionist's job was to maintain an orderly, fair queue.

The assignment of clients to intake workers was facilitated by the entry of names on a checkerboard chart. The intake workers' names were listed in a column down the left-hand side of the chart. As each client arrived, his or her name was placed below the name of the last client to arrive, alongside the name of the next intake worker down the list. As each column was completed, the next name was placed at the top of the next column to the right. Thus, clients were assigned to intake workers and the queue was ordered by filling in the next chart according to the rule "top to bottom, left to right." This procedure, and the chart of the day's activities it created, were the accountable way of assigning clients to workers in this agency.

The receptionists were accountable to follow that procedure as well as to keep an orderly, fair queue of clients. Occasionally, these two practical interests —to maintain a fair, orderly queue and to follow established procedure—conflicted. Intake workers regularly confronted cases that took markedly longer than average. This created an exceptionally long wait for the intake workers' waiting clients. During the long wait, people who arrived later but were assigned to a quicker intake worker, were served ahead of the delayed worker's clients. Although procedure was being followed, the principle of first come, first served had been violated. To reestablish an orderly queue, the rule had to be temporarily modified, and so it was. The receptionist reassigned the slow worker's clients to others, erased and changed the chart, and corrected the records of the altered assignments. The purpose of the rule was served by violating the rule. At the same time, the correction of the charts and records made it difficult to keep track of how often the rule needed suspension. This protected the rule itself from scrutiny as a possible problem.

Consideration of this type of conflict points out another aspect of commonsense reasoning. When trouble is caused by one person's pursuit of conflicting interests, it is resolved by establishing priorities among them. The neglect or undermining of one task is justified by the priority of another. The order of priorities is not necessarily discretionary. Receptionists, for example, may be accountable to recognize when exceptions to the rule are justified by circumstances and to avoid trouble by making exceptions. That is, the receptionists may be accountable to achieve two ends and to correctly judge when one must be sacrificed to the other.[5]

A second point must be made about this type of conflict. Accountability to follow routinized procedures conditioned the solutions of problems caused by those procedures. Notice that the solution to the conflict between maintaining an orderly queue and following routinized procedures included correcting the chart and records so that the appearance of having followed routine procedures was maintained in the written record. Elsewhere, queues are ordered by taking numbers, by forming lines, by making appointments in advance, by giving crisis cases priority, and by matching the waiting clients to workers as workers become available. Combinations of these methods are also used. For example, many banks preserve the first-come, first-served order by forming a line of customers and sending the next customer to the first available teller. In effect, tellers are assigned to customers instead of the reverse. This is not a suggestion to improve agency operations. There are probably good reasons why some or all of these would not work. For example, waiting to assign clients until the next worker is ready might lead to problems in record-keeping. What is important is that none of these other procedures is tried. Problems are handled in a way that honors the various practical interests in the setting, including the ones that are temporarily suspended.[6]

Other practical conflicts are generated by accountability to a routine procedure. On one occasion, a client expressed preference for one intake worker over another. The two workers switched cases to accommodate the preference.

---

[5]   Merton (1968) argues that competent task performance regularly includes recognizing the priority of ends over routinized means. To subvert ends by inappropriately ahereing to standardized procedures is accountable as a form of deviance. The boundaries of "appropriate" adherence to procedure are loosely defined. Merton argues that the distribution of power, knowledge, and involvement help resolve differences over their placement.

[6]   The simultaneous expression of conflicting interests in behavior may be very general indeed. Monkeys were trained to self-administer cocaine by pulling a lever with one hand; they were also trained to interrupt the availability of the cocaine by pulling a second lever with the other hand. Once trained, they pulled the lever that provided cocaine with increasing rapidity while at the same time pulling the lever to interrupt their supply of cocaine with increasing rapidity (Spealman 1979). That is, the monkeys acted simultaneously on two directly conflicting tasks and did not develop the more efficient approach of using only the lever that administered the cocaine, but more slowly. The simultaneous honoring of conflicting tasks may be a very primitive aspect of our ability to resolve problems, one that is not even restricted to our species.

No delay was caused by switching the two cases, but the chart and records had to be corrected and the rule of procedure was violated. Priority was given to avoiding trouble that might arise from denying the request over both the rule of procedure and the trouble of altering the charts and records. Avoiding trouble in the form of the client's possible reaction was another sense of what is implied by maintaining an orderly queue.

Still another conflict was observed. One intake worker had special interest and facility in handling difficult cases. The difficult cases were assigned to that worker as the cases arrived, contradicting the routine procedure. This was a problem-solving arrangement, but it operated as a standing and accountable, if informal, rule. The simple procedural rule "top to bottom, left to right" turned out to be not so simple after all. To it we must add the exceptions: unless an intake worker was delayed enough to cause trouble; unless someone had a strong enough preference that denying it might cause trouble; unless everyone's day could be made easier by assigning all the problem cases to one worker; etc.

"Etc." implies that additional unanticipated problems may arise that call for alteration of the routine procedure. When they do arise, the rule is understood to include those new problems, whatever they are, as exceptions. In following the rule, everyone is expected to accountably recognize exceptions and deal with them appropriately. Every commonsense rule of conduct, every routine, every loose category has a list of exceptions, including unspecified "etc." "Etc." is a formal property of commonsense reasoning. Every commonsense statement is understood to refer to things that cannot be specified in advance but that one must reconcile, as they arise, with that statement.

Reconciling Contradictory Norms Held by Different Groups

Wedow (1979) studied the experience of paranoia and the use of that term among college students who used illegal drugs during the 1960s. The drug user faced a chronic conflict of practical interests. On the one hand, for consciousness expansion, relaxation, countercultural value expression, group affiliation, or what have you, the user wanted to use drugs. Maybe the user just wanted to get high. On the other hand, mere possession of the drugs, let along buying or selling them, was a crime. The drug users Wedow studied were members of groups that advocated drug use. Group values supported and reinforced the interest in drugs. But membership in a subcultural group does not reduce one's accountability to the law. Although there are many people who disapprove of marijuana smoking, the only ones with practical relevance are those who are expected to express their disapproval with sanctions. In effect, then, the practically relevant representatives of the law and conventional morality are the police.

This conflict of practical interests is different from the ones found in the public assistance agency. In the agency, the conflict of interests was shared by various employees, and the priorities by which they were resolved were also shared. In this situation, however, the conflict between practical interests was created by the simultaneous accountability of the drug users to two social groups that did not agree upon the proper course of conduct. The preference of the drug user for one group and its values did not reduce the user's accountability to the other group. Once one had committed oneself to violating the law, the sensible course of action was to avoid arrest and prosecution. This is the practical task that drug users set for themselves. They tried to restrict their illegal activities in ways that reduced the likelihood that they would come to the attention of the police.

In this task, the drug users observed Pynchon's (1973) fourth Proverb for Paranoids as a rule of conduct: "You hide, they seek."[7] For the drug users, the relevant seekers were the police, from whom illegal activities were hidden as well as could be. Concealment was complicated by the desire to use drugs in relatively public places and to appear in public places under the influence of the drugs. As Pynchon (1973) puts it in his fifth Proverb for Paranoids, "Paranoids are not paranoid because they are paranoid, but because they keep putting themselves, fucking idiots, deliberately into paranoid situations."

Two assumptions about the realities of police surveillance further complicated the drug users' task. First, the police were believed to use the laws against drugs as a convenient tool for controlling other activities, such as radical politics, which were not illegal in themselves. Engaging in politics or other behavior that the police frowned upon was believed to give the police an interest in one's activities. The interest was expressed by singling out people who were disliked for prosecution under the drug laws. This belief, true or not, was a reasonable one. We have already seen that the police acted in exactly this manner when arresting skid-row inhabitants. Second, the police were believed to employ undercover agents. This reduced the utility of the marked police car and the police uniform as signs that surveillance was being conducted. The drug users had to be alert to the possible danger of arrest in ordinary-looking situations.

In the process of concealment, paranoia was a term used to classify situations by the threat of exposure that they posed and feelings by the level of experienced danger and anxiety. In a web of exceptions and qualifications, courses of action that violated good hiding procedure were justified. However, mindfulness of danger was also exhibited in the recognition that one was feeling paranoid or that the situation was a paranoid one.

One hiding procedure was to conduct drug-oriented activities only in trusted settings and among trusted people. Strangers were regarded warily in incriminating circumstances. But strangers introduced and vouched for by friends were granted quick intimacy. A rule for drug dealing was to sell only to friends. If they wanted to act as go-betweens, obtaining marijuana for third parties, that was cool. If that rule were followed, dealers would never do business with

---

[7]   Goffman (1959) refers to the variety of practices this norm generates as "audience segregation" and "impression management."

strangers. But that rule was frequently relaxed to permit friends to bring dealers and customers together. Relaxing the rule, however, increased paranoia.

Marijuana smoking was occasionally done in open, public places. This contradicted rules of practice that restricted smoking to secure environments. One's home and friends' homes were the most secure environments. Holding the cigarette out of sight and passing it inconspicuously made concerts and political gatherings acceptably secure. At outdoor concerts, a good view of the surrounding area and distance from others sufficed. Still, these situations were somewhat paranoid.

Despite the lack of uniforms, drug users may have felt that they were able to recognize undercover police. This confidence, of course, overrode the concern about the presence of strangers when drug-related activities were occurring. Informants were unable to tell how they recognized the police, but they remained certain that they could. The willingness to expose one's illegal activities to strangers was also fostered by reciprocal incrimination. Hearing another talk about drugs made him or her vulnerable and justified reciprocal intimacy. Still, there were doubts that one had judged strangers too quickly and had acted too openly in their presence.

Finally, there was the matter of "passing" while high. Once in public, the drug users did their best to appear normal and to avoid calling attention to themselves. Still, there was always the doubt that one looked strange or was acting strangely. Passing was aided by actively avoiding activities that threatened one's composure. One informant found it difficult to interact with her mother while taking LSD. This became an ordeal to be avoided if possible.

Two practical tasks, then, using illegal drugs and avoiding arrest, came into conflict. The reconciliation of the opposing pressures on the drug user took the form of attempting to restrict illegal activities to safe situations in which detection by the police was unlikely. The primary rules for hiding seemed to be (1) do not compromise yourself in the presence of strangers and (2) restrict drug usage to secure environments, especially one's own home and the homes of friends. These two rules reduced paranoia to a minimum, if followed. But a number of exceptions to the rule were allowed, and these resulted in situations of varying degrees of paranoia. In avoiding arrest and taking care of business, then, degrees of paranoia denote how well business was being taken care of.

Wedow's study revealed some interesting aspects of the use of social norms. First, important and consequential norms admit to accountable exceptions. In this, they are similar to the relatively simple norm for maintaining a queue in the public assistance agency. Second, there is a vocabulary for communicating practical information about activities to others who share one's interests. To exchange anecdotes about paranoid situations is to instruct one another about situations with noteworthy danger. Third, in this complex situation, complicated practical wisdom develops about when people can be trusted, about when surveillance is likely, and about other matters of practical concern.

Finally, where different groups are expected to differently evaluate a course of conduct, people contrive to control information in ways that respect the power and opinions of each group. Notice the similarities between the responses of the drug users and those of the pieceworkers. Both systematically concealed information from those who might use it against them.

Using Conflicting Applicable Norms

Users of illegal drugs are subject to two sets of contradictory norms. Each set, however, is pressed upon the users by an identifiable group. Drug users regard the problem of deciding which set of norms is applicable in a situation as an empirical question. The drug users follow the norms of their own group unless scrutiny of the scene suggests that the law may be enforced. In such cases, drug use becomes secretive or is suspended, depending on the degree of perceived danger. The drug users do not perceive their situation as one in which they can choose among sets of norms. Rather, the appropriate norms, whether preferred or not, are imposed by the nature of the audience.

Complex social arrangements, for example, the operation of a piecework shop, can continue despite thorough differences between different participants' understanding of events. In the piecework shop, the workers' production was interpreted in terms of two distinct economic analyses of the piecework incentives and two distinct opinions of the workers' comprehension of their circumstances. Events in the shop simultaneously supported both interpretations, and no one but the researcher seemed particularly aware of the discrepancies. Thus, although diverse interpretations were present in the shop, they were not present in a way that allowed people in the shop to choose between them.

Wieder's study of a halfway house for drug addicts (1974) documents the organization of social life around two contradictory sets of norms and interpretative assumptions that are both available as choices to the participants. One set of norms and interpretive assumptions was found in the official regulations of the halfway house. The second set was found in the "convict code." The convict code was a group of norms of inmate conduct, developed by inmates themselves, that are found in many institutions.

The halfway house staff, of course, had greater allegiance to the official rules than did the residents. But both groups utilized both sets of norms. The staff assumed inmate compliance with the code as a condition to be considered in their own plans, and the residents could violate the code in favor of the official rules when that was convenient. In the halfway house, then, sustaining an orderly routine involved utilizing two contradictory sets of rules and assumptions, either of which might be used by any participant.

As part of the rehabilitation program, residents were required to avoid drugs and to aid the staff by providing information about backsliders. The convict code, to the contrary, included the rule "Do not snitch." Each of these rules was believed to be enforced by sanctions. The staff was understood to grant privileges and favorable official evaluations for compliance with house rules. Residents who snitched were believed to receive violent punishment from those on whom they snitched. Staff members were fully aware of the bind this created for the inmates. Staff members were reminded of the code and the severity of its enforcement. The staff relaxed its promotion of house rules in acknowledgment that the code had priority, despite their own preferences. Thus, the staff oriented to the code as a social reality as did the residents.

In the self-protecting manner of commonsense arrangements, staff acknowledgment of the code supported a reduction of their efforts to get residents to follow the official regulations. This made the code seem stronger and perpetuated its use. By assuming that the code would be enforced and that it was pointless to pressure residents to violate it, and then by reducing their efforts in the face of this assumed reality, the staff actually increased the relevance of the code. Here, again, we see that commonsense arrangements are preserved by unquestioned continuation of habitual routines. We see, too, that people are able to orient themselves to assumptions about how others will act and to accommodate themselves to assumed powerlessness against that reality.

Providing information to the researcher was treated by the residents and the researchers as akin to snitching. The residents would not discuss certain topics. When questioned, they were evasive, and they attributed their evasion to the code. Thus, the evasion was not a personal affront but, rather, was dictated by the reality of the code. Wieder found that, like staff members, he must acknowledge the code and the limitations it placed on available information. Wieder reasoned that, if he pressed the residents on issues that they did not wish to discuss, his relationship with them would suffer and he would get no information at all. Thus, the code was acknowledged as a condition of the research. Although Wieder was aware of the code as a set of untested assumptions, he was nonetheless led to acknowledge its reality.

In general, when resident behavior was explained by reference to the code, the chosen course of action was given priority over available alternatives. For, if the code was involved, so were severe sanctions. Thus, if a staff member could be convinced that the code demanded some conduct, that member would be likely to diminish his or her efforts to alter that conduct. There was nothing in the staff's arsenal of sanctions to rival the severity of the violent punishment that was believed to enforce the code.[8] Further, behavior demanded by the code

---

[8]   When violence did occur among residents, it was to their advantage to attribute the violence to the demands of the code. The code, in general, demanded violent retribution against wrongdoers to prevent further abuses. The official penalties for violence might not be reduced, but by referring to the code the violence was rendered more routine and explicable and less personal. One's official reputation, as recorded in the files, would be less affected than it would be by violence not demanded by the code. One's reputation among fellow residents also remained more businesslike. Incidentally, attributing violence to the code, whatever its causes, would provide evidence of the code's reality and of the residents' commitment to it. This would make the code less likely to be challenged as an explanation for any conduct and more likely to be offered as an explanation. The reality of the code existed in this web of uses to which it could be put.

did not reflect personal feelings. Refusing to snitch, for example, was no insult to staff or researcher. Other exchanges of favors were not disqualified. In the same way, official rules could be used to depersonalize what the staff "had to do." For example, an inmate could refuse to snitch and a staff member could officially sanction that inmate without disturbing otherwise amicable relations between them.

Staff awareness of the code entered into problem-solving activities. Balance was sought between the demands of the official regulations and the code. For example, the staff interpreted its own responsibilities for the regulation of inmate relationships in light of the code. If one inmate stole another's watch, staff did not think the victim should snitch and involve them in the case. Instead, the victim should find the culprit and administer justice according to the code. The consequences of snitching were believed to be so severe that the staff recommended against officially proper action that involved snitching. Here, the assumption of the code's operation led staff to preclude certain options by withdrawing their support from inmates who violated the code to follow official policy. Then, inmates' following of the code was taken as evidence that the staff attitude was justified.

On other occasions, group loyalty was asserted by residents by following the code. Inmates pressured one another to use drugs and interpreted drug use as a commitment to the code and to the group of residents. The presence of the code seemed to make following the official regulations, in many instances, a sign of a personal choice in favor of staff over residents. Staff, then, put up with undesirable behavior because they assumed that the inmates could not violate the code with impunity. Staff may have even lost respect for code violators. Staff willingness to accept misconduct without protest further strengthened the code by disarming official alternatives to it. When inmates weighed their practical interests, staff support of the code enabled them to disregard official regulations to the extent that the staff accepted the code as the appropriate guide for resident conduct.

As the code depersonalized resident conduct, it also depersonalized staff failures. Difficulties in maintaining discipline or relating to the residents did not reflect on staff competence if they could be attributed to the code. For example, group therapy was rejected by inmates. The explanation that group therapy violated the code mitigated the staff's failure to motivate the residents. Staff responsibilities and planning of various kinds were evaluated with acknowledgment of the effects of the code. In general, staff was able to justify reduced efforts on its part, and the failure of various programs, by showing that the code was implicated in residents' reluctance to participate.

By focusing on the operation of the code, I do not mean to minimize the role of the official regulations. Residents may have acted up and have resisted official regulation, but they did not, for example, just leave. Staff members may have lowered their expectations for success, but they did not abandon all efforts. We have been discussing various exceptions and qualifications of the official regulations as they applied to both staff and resident responsibilities. They are noteworthy because these exceptions and qualifications were organized around a set of informal rules, acknowledged by all parties as an assumed reality. Balancing the demands of the code against the demands of official rules, then, became a complex task for all participants. Staff and residents had to evaluate both sets of demands, anticipate one another's course of conduct, choose a course of action, and justify it in terms of one or the other set of norms. Choice of a normative system allowed much conduct to be depersonalized. Resident's use of the code was made more comfortable, or possible, by staff's willingness to recognize the code as a real consideration. Staff recognition of the code justified delegation of discipline to the informal system, reduced effort in projects countermanded by the code, and failure of efforts to reach the residents.

Two normative systems, then, were acknowledged by all participants in the halfway house. The activities in the setting were oriented to both sets of rules. The presence of two sets of rules organized the exceptions and qualifications to each in terms of the other. In addition, the relative weight given to the two sets of rules supported complex judgments of group loyalty, personal involvement, and so on. Formally, the rules operated like the other rules we have discussed. We can see, however, that multiple interpretive assumptions and rules of conduct can be supported in an ongoing situation. In pursuit of their practical interests, people are able to orient their conduct to the multiple sets of rules and to use them to interpret events and guide the conduct of others in a favorable manner.

Dealing with Unpleasant Realities

Emerson and Pollner (1976) studied the activities of psychiatric emergency teams (PET). They reported on an aspect of PET work that was unpleasant and counter to the normative values of the psychiatric community. Still, the work was a routine part of the PET job and was required by the demands of the work situation. It was recognized to be necessary, even though it was normatively deviant. PET members found themselves routinely doing work that was contrary to their professional values and accounted for it as "dirty work." Denigrating the work was routinized in the setting. This denigration served to maintain values even when violations of them were routine and required. It also indicated that not all accountable behavior is normative, even when it is a routine part of situations. The norm governing this work seemed to be to do it and to complain about it. Complaints, it seems, can be routinized in a setting and may serve the function of preserving the very conduct the complaints are about.

PET work typically began in response to a call alerting them to a psychiatric emergency. Usually, these calls were not placed by the person with the problem but rather by his or her family, neighbors, landlord, and so on. The calls amounted to complaints about a person or a request that something be done for or about him or her. In many of these cases, no recognizable therapy could be done and the situation dictated that coercion be used to control the client. This combination of being unable to do anything for the clients and being forced to do something to them was regarded as dirty work by PET members. The cases may have been psychiatrically hopeless or clients may not have been willing to cooperate after having been brought to the attention of the authorities. Nothing could be done for them except to hospitalize them, and when there was little therapeutic hope, hospitalization was regarded as coercive control: doing to patients, not for them.

In PET work, hospitalization was frequent due to the nature of the clients. By defining coercive hospitalization as dirty work, PET workers affirmed that neither they nor their position was to be judged by it. No matter how frequently it occurred, dirty work was always an exception to the normatively preferred means of handling problems. It was used only when the situation required it. The situation of an unwilling client (with a poor psychiatric prognosis) reported by others and of a limited number of programs to utilize as resources frequently dictated hospitalization as a necessary step. Complaining about that aspect of PET work, constantly reaffirming the norms it violated, served to preserve the preferred, noncoercive definition of psychiatric practice. At the same time, it preserved favorable identities for PET workers. It suggested their knowledge and commitment to the norms as a standard of judgment rather than as the exceptional dirty work forced upon them by practicing therapy in a restricted bureaucratic environment.

The complaints about the work may also have contributed to the self-concealing procedures that preserved that work as a routine. By treating each instance of coercion as an exception, the frequency of coercion did not become an issue. The conflict between the norms governing therapy and the actions that therapists were routinely required to take did not lead to confrontation. Therapists did not feel obligated to resist the demands that ran counter to their professional norms; the employers of therapists did not feel obligated to insist that professional standards be reformulated to be more realistic. By attaching a routinized negative evaluation to aspects of the work, everyone involved could accept the work, taken as a whole, as reasonably reflecting professional norms and the practical demands of actual practice situations. Employers could feel that therapists did what was required, even if they did complain a lot; therapists could feel that they were honoring their professional standards, even if they had to do a lot of demeaning dirty work. Complaints about bad aspects of the work functioned, at least in this setting, to emphasize the overall higher quality of the work. This protected the routine from negative evaluation and preserved it. In general, regular, institutionalized complaints may preserve the arrangement they complain about.

Mutatis Mutandis and Ceteris Paribus—
Two More Formal Properties

We have already discussed two formal properties of categories and rules in the commonsense attitude—"etc." and "let it pass." Like them, *mutatis mutandis* and *ceteris paribus* are specifications of how loose or indexical expressions are used and understood. The terms are in Latin because they have been useful since Latin was the language of all scholarship. Latin is still widely used in the terminology of law, medicine, biology, and philosophy, and Latin phrases developed in those disciplines are seldom translated. In addition, terms from other languages, especially French and German, are also frequently incorporated into sociological terminology. Do not be intimidated by these foreign phrases. It is not necessary to know the languages of their origins to understand their use as technical terms. When you encounter these terms, treat them as you would any other term with which you are unfamiliar: look them up in a dictionary. Unabridged dictionaries include almost all the foreign terms that are in general sociological use. There are also several specialized dictionaries that provide translations of commonly used foreign words and phrases. All the foreign terms in this book, for example, are translated adequately in Mawson (1975). Elementary logic textbooks are good sources for Latin expressions referring to forms of argument or formal characteristics of expressions. A librarian should be able to quickly locate the best sources available in your library.

Mutatis mutandis is a Latin idiom that means that all necessary changes have been made or that details have been altered appropriately for the situation. Suppose that every morning you eat sugared ChocoCrunchems for breakfast. One morning, woe the luck, you are out of ChocoCrunchems. *Mutatis mutandis,* you alter your plans to accommodate this detail and eat something else.

Every commonsense rule is understood to apply to situations, *mutatis mutandis.* Minor variations in a situation are expected to occur and are expected to be accompanied by minor variations in conduct that have not been specified in advance by the rule. This is closely related to the notion that rules are always understood to include unspecified exceptions and qualifications, indicated by the term "etc." When an event occurs that is not specified in the rule, but is not a significant enough change to make the rule inapplicable, people are expected to follow the rule by making the appropriate corrections in their behavior. Thus, when the receptionist in the public assistance agency reassigned clients to avoid unfair waiting for a slow intake worker, she was following the rules *mutatis mutandis.* When marijuana smoking occurred in paranoid places, the joint was passed secretively. The various ways in which the joint was concealed, each responsive to the nature and intensity of surveillance in the particular situation, were variations on "passing the joint," *mutatis mutandis.* When members of a therapy group were uncooperative because an informal code of conduct prohibited enthusiastic participation, staff members lowered their expectations for the group. These lowered expectations were appropriate, professional expectations, *mutatis mutandis.*

Several English idioms are reasonably close to *mutatis mutandis* in meaning. When instructions or regulations prove inadequate, people "wing it." They "fly by the seats of their pants." They "play it by ear." They "go with the flow." They "scope it out and keep it cool." They cope. They improvise. They "catch as catch can." They "play it as it lays." When life hands them a lemon, they make lemonade. They get by on getting by. They follow ordinary procedure, *mutatis mutandis.*

Ceteris paribus has an English idiomatic translation: "all things being equal." Commonsense rules of conduct are understood to apply, all things being equal. For example, all things being equal, assigning clients to intake workers by filling out the prearranged chart should produce an orderly queue. But all things are not always equal. Sometimes intake workers have time-consuming cases; sometimes clients prefer one intake worker to another; sometimes an intake worker specializes in difficult cases; and so on. When these unequal conditions occur, the specific rule no longer applies in its precise form. Instead, it applies *mutatis mutandis,* and the receptionist is expected to adapt the procedure to the realities of the instance.

There is a convenient order to these four formal properties. Rules of conduct are specified and apply in the specified form, all things being equal or *ceteris paribus.* However, events occur that are not specified in advance but are not so disruptive as to completely disqualify the rule. These events are expected to occur, and the rule is understood to include them when they occur. These events are referred to as "etc.," unspecified variations, and people are expected to handle them appropriately. Learning to handle these events is often called "learning the ropes." Since rules are understood to include unspecified variations, rule following must include appropriate accommodation of conduct to these variations. The rule is followed *mutatis mutandis.* The various judgments involved are necessarily done on the spot (*ad hoc*) and creatively. The operation of the formal property "let it pass" allows variations to be employed without undue challenge and disruption.

SUMMARY

Most generally, the ethnomethodological program is to specify the formal structure of everyday talk and action. Philosophical analyses drew attention to reflexivity, indexicality, the commonsense attitude, and the documentary method of interpretation as the crucial topics for study. These served as starting points for ethnomethodological study.

The commonsense attitude includes the maintenance of a variety of assumptions about the world. These assumptions are protected from scrutiny by standardized commonsense arrangements and are resistant to study. However, if these assumptions fail to work satisfactorily, if the environment becomes senseless and problem-solving procedures fail to restore the sense of its order, the commonsense attitude itself becomes a problem and is made visible for study. Abandonment of the commonsense attitude as a temporary response to confusion and senseless events is called a breach of that attitude.

Many of the earliest ethnomethodological studies were environmental manipulations designed to produce breaches. As the phenomena became more clearly defined, less drastic means of gathering data were employed. Naturally occurring breaches were studied. By a naturally occurring breach I mean a situation that occurs naturally, without manipulation by the researcher, and which so thoroughly contradicts our everyday assumptions that it provokes attention to the commonsense attitude. Agnes's life as a transsexual is the most striking example. In addition, improved understanding of the commonsense attitude permits gentler manipulations, such as the psychiatric interview study. These manipulations were successful in making accounting activities easily available for study, but without breaching the commonsense attitude. Still other studies were able to demonstrate important characteristics of accounting activities in routine problem-solving activities in natural settings. For example, the activities of receptionists in keeping an orderly queue demonstrated the need to amend even simple rules as unanticipated contingencies arose.

Practical interests provide the underlying pattern to people's activities. In their everyday activities, people consider events in terms of how their achievement of goals will be affected and respond to events in ways that can best be understood as attempts to achieve practical goals. Multiple goals are typically pursued simultaneously, so much of practical reasoning involves reassessing priorities among one's various goals or reassessing the effectiveness of routine procedures in the light of unanticipated events. A fundamental, standing goal is to preserve one's sense that events are proceeding in an orderly way. In pursuit of this goal, people amend rules of conduct to fit them to unanticipated contingencies rather than discarding or reformulating them. Further, people expect one another to understand the rules flexibly enough to adapt them to new events. The way in which rules and categories are adapted to new events provides evidence of their formal characteristics.

Rules and statements are not understood literally and they are not understood to be complete. Rather, people are expected to qualify and amend them as needed. Rules are understood to apply as formulated, all things being equal (*ceteris paribus*). When all things are not equal, the conduct specified in the rule or the definition of the categories becomes inappropriate. People are expected to recognize when this occurs and make appropriate allowance and changes. That is, they are expected to apply the rule *mutatis mutandis*. It is understood that the expression of a rule is incomplete and that a fuller expression would include a variety of anticipated exceptions and qualifications. In addition, people expect unpredictable events to occur. These are indicated by the term "etc." Finally, people "let it pass." They forgive surprises and misgivings so long as they are acceptable variations for the purpose at hand. This reduces the number of challenges to creative solutions to practical problems and to the rules themselves.

This formal structure supports a variety of uses for rules of conduct and categories. It also supports the maintenance of routine arrangements despite conflicts of practical interests and the presence of diverse interpretations of events among the participants in a social arrangement. The reasoning in ethnomethodological studies can now be summarized. First, the major practical interests of the people being studied must be identified. These need not be articulated by the people themselves, but they must be adequately identified, in the sense that the people behave as if they pursued those interests. Second, conduct and practical reasoning is demonstrated to be related to those interests. By observing how people respond to conflicts of interests, unanticipated events, and their own assumptions about how others will behave, the formal structure of their reasoning is made visible. Various uses of terms can be compared; the amendment of rules to meet new contingencies can be studied.

Wedow's study of paranoia among drug users illustrates this model well. First, two conflicting practical interests are identified: the use of illegal drugs and the avoidance of arrest. Second, a variety of routine behaviors and terminology is related to those interests. Among them are wariness of strangers and confining activities to secure environments. The term paranoia is understood as a report of how well the avoidance of arrest is being pursued. Paranoid situations are situations in which one is conducting oneself in a manner that raises anxiety that one will be arrested or otherwise harrassed. Finally, the application of basic rules of hiding is shown to have the formal properties we have discussed.

A FORMAL EXERCISE

To this point, you have practiced reporting single episodes of behavior. Even in these trivial episodes, you probably experienced difficulty in describing them to others clearly. Now, try your hand at describing more complex events. First, pick a setting that you can observe. Again, make it a public place. You may be a participant in the setting, but do not abuse your access to private information. Take notes of what you observe in the setting. In class discussions, try to make sense of the notes as a whole rather than as episodic units. Try to describe events in the setting, or some selected theme, using your notes to answer your classmates' questions. Work at the descriptions until they satisfy people as a good account of your notes or until it is clear that you need to observe further. Stretching the discussions over a few weeks should allow ongoing note-taking to be guided in response to the questions of others. Later, if it is assigned, or if you would like to do one for other reasons, the notes can be the basis of an original, ethnomethodological study.

SUGGESTED READINGS

Any of the studies discussed or cited in this chapter is recommended. Additional original studies are conveniently gathered by Douglas (1970) and Turner (1974). Pollner (1974; 1975) discusses many of the important theoretical issues suggested in this book in detail. Moerman (1966), Wieder and Zimmerman (1974; 1976), and Stoddart (1974) present short empirical studies that provide further illustration of how ethnomethodology is done. Sanders (1977) contains a more extended and detailed study.

5

Practical Reasoning in Measurement and Categorizing

Chapters 3 and 4 were concerned with elaborating the formal structure of practical reasoning—its rules of inference and argument. We took people's accounts very seriously, treating the verbal accounts as arguments and treating actions and decisions as reasoned responses to complex practical interests. We assumed that the reasoning was correct or, more precisely, correct enough for the practical situation in which it occurred. Instead of standing in judgment of people's conclusions and reasoning, we granted their adequacy. With judgment suspended, it is possible to study how the reasoning is done.

It became clear that accounts cannot be taken literally or manipulated in a strict, traditionally logical way. People anticipate that exceptions will occur. Terms are employed and rules are followed in ways that take these exceptions into account. People also expect others to make exceptions and to accommodate themselves to exceptions that are thrust upon them. These expectations are sanctioned, too. Accounts prove to be reflexive, fully explicable only in the context of the situation in which they occur. Accounts are influenced by the practical tasks of the moment and the priorities among them. The accommodation of plans to new and shifting priorities prove to be among the central concerns of all practical reasoning.

In all the discussions, the availability of sensible accounts was taken for granted. About how events are categorized, about how people transform raw events into accounts, I have said little. And that little has been that the categorization process is self-concealing. People do not scrupulously investigate factual assertions, even when important decisions are based on them. Instead, they rely upon untested assumptions. The right to use unquestioned assumptions is defended by sanctions. The freedom from challenge by others is protected by sanctions as well.

Categorization, or perception, will not be treated as an independent process that provides categorized information for further manipulation (reasoning or cognition). Instead, prior knowledge and the reasoning process influence perception. Practical reasoning, and the untested assumptions it employs, influence the collection and categorization of the information that serves as evidence in the ongoing reasoning process. As traditional logic served as a point of departure for the study of practical reasoning, scientific measurement serves as the point of departure for the study of categorizing.

WHY SCIENTIFIC MEASUREMENT IS
AN ATTRACTIVE POINT OF DEPARTURE

Science stands in an odd, almost paradoxical, relationship to practical reasoning and practical affairs. On the one hand, scientific rigor is especially respected, trusted, and sought in the assembly of information for practical decisions. In this context, science is regarded as an exceptionally careful and accurate, and therefore valuable, species of practical fact finding. In this sense, science is more highly valued for supporting engineering that for supporting theory.

On the other hand, the rigor and precision of the scientific measurement, and of the interpretation of data, are often claimed to be different from commonsense observation and interpretation. In this context, the scientific method is claimed to replace common sense. The peculiarities of everyday observation and reasoning are regarded as flawed or mistaken attempts to be rational. Science is regarded as a successful attempt to be rational, one that replaces everyday practices of observation and reasoning with more adequate ones. The proper role of science, then, is not to serve as a source of information to be utilized in practical decisions. Instead, science is expected to ultimately replace our practical decision-making apparatus with a more scientifically sound one.

These are not two competitive views of science. The paradoxical status of science in practical affairs is generated by the fact that the very precision that makes science a desirable tool of practical decision making also justifies the claim that science should replace other approaches to practical decision making.[1] It is not uncommon to find these two views of science espoused by the same people as each, in turn, suits the occasion.

Ethnomethodologists have empirically addressed two kinds of questions about science. Studies have been done to determine how scientific findings are actually employed in practical decision making. We will discuss a representative study by Leiter (1974; 1976) that shows that the formal characteristics of practical decision-making, especially the interpretation of particular facts by consulting contextual information, is not changed by the scientific status of some of the facts. Ethnomethodologists argue that practical reasoning is present whenever sense-making occurs. The gathering of some facts by scientific procedures does not create an exception.

Another group of studies has been done to determine whether scientific measurement itself is fundamentally different from commonsense observation and categorization. Does the scientific method replace practical reasoning or is practical reasoning an unnoticed, self-concealing part of scientific measurement as it seems to be in everyday life? The special status of scientific investigations does not depend on their being formally unique. They might be loose, considered technically, but still worthy of such superior confidence that the distinction from common sense is justified. Practically, then, the level of confidence is more important than formal structure except when the topic being studied is accounts or reasoning. Then formal structure is crucial.

Background assumptions are widely recognized to enter into several im-

---

[1] The collision of scientific and political institutions over control of policy is quite public with respect to two current issues: the limitation of recombinant DNA research and nuclear power. The controversy over the testing of pharmaceuticals is another, less publicized, battleground.

portant aspects of science. The definition of problems for research is largely determined by norms and conventions in the scientific community. Scientific communities support normative assumptions about the nature of the world. These assumptions suggest problems for research and also discourage consideration of other problems. They are also conditions of what may be said about the problems and how research can be done. (See Kuhn 1957; 1962 and Toulmin 1961 for examples.)

Beliefs in the society at large are also influential in guiding scientific research. In our country, for example, the beliefs of politicians about what topics need study affects the availability of funds for research and training. The roller-coaster demand for engineers as our space program moves in and out of political favor is an interesting example. Surges in research funds for particular topics greatly affect the distribution of research interests, especially when expensive equipment and training are required for research. Medical research, which requires expensive facilities, is greatly affected by political decisions between, for example, focusing research on a single disease such as cancer or supporting good research on any topic. High-energy physics and astronomy require massive, expensive equipment, which, in turn, requires years to design and build. Long-term political and financial commitments, then, are instrumental in the practice of science.

But none of these practical concerns reflects directly on measurement. After the financial and political maneuvering is completed, after the conventions of the scientific community have shaped the research problem, it may still be possible to enter the laboratory and conduct one's observations in a way that adheres so strictly to the scientific method that practical considerations do not intrude. To my knowledge, no ethnomethodological studies of the actual measurement practices in the physical sciences have been conducted. However, studies have been done on measurement in the social sciences. Cicourel's (1964; 1968; 1974a) pioneering work indicates that practical reasoning is directly implicated in social scientific measurement.

The importance of practical reasoning in scientific measurement becomes clear if one remembers Lewis Carroll's proof that logical deduction requires assumptions that cannot be explicated in the rules of logic. These assumptions are necessary to recognize and accept that the steps in a logical argument are adequately clear and explicit, that a proof has actually been accomplished. Between each step in a proof there is a leap of faith. Implicit assumptions remain a part of every proof, no matter how explicit it becomes. The adequacy of the proof depends upon one's willingness to accept these implicit assumptions and to make these leaps of faith. What is true of traditional syllogistic logic is true of other formal systems. Carroll's proof, then, is a very important support for the contention that practical or commonsense assumptions are part of all sense-making activities. We may impose formal systems on our reasoning, but these formal systems do not replace practical reasoning. It remains, implicitly, in every step of the explicit reasoning.

The claim that scientific measurement can replace commonsense observation parallels the claim that explicit formal systems can replace practical reasoning. But the validity of that claim must be established empirically as well as by analytic reasoning. Analytic reasoning can establish that all empirical categories, including those used in scientific measurement, are loose or indexical. But loose or indexical categories are not necessarily imprecise. Empirical judgments can be made with great confidence under certain conditions, and empirical categories can be manipulated logically without error when they have been applied correctly. Whether categories are used precisely enough is a judgment that can only be made when the purposes of the measurement are known.

One practical purpose to which scientific measurement can be put is to serve as data for ethnomethodological study. A question is raised, then, that must be addressed empirically. Scientists are prepared to accept that their measurements are governed by the explicit rules of science. For their purposes, practical reasoning does not appear. But can practical reasoning be exhibited by ethnomethodological study, for its purposes?

Scientific measurement is precise enough to pass the inspection of scientists and precise enough to support elaborate theoretical and engineering applications. It is possible, very possible, that measurement in some areas of science is so precise that ethnomethodologists cannot find the influence of practical reasoning. In such cases, we might know indirectly, by analytic reasoning and by our knowledge of how perception works, that practical reasoning must be present. But, at the same time, we would have to acknowledge that, for our purposes, it cannot be shown to be present. That is, we cannot find it.

The issue, then, is not confined to formal structure. There is also the question of whether the ability to be careful and precise and to follow scientific procedure is more developed than the ability to recognize the intrusion of practical reasoning despite the procedure. Practical reasoning in the social sciences is not so resistant to discovery, however.

Finally, the study of scientific measurement helps put the observation of other settings into a useful perspective. Science imposes procedures and vocabulary on its practitioners. As we shall see, practical reasoning is involved in applying these explicit rules and categories in the social sciences. Whatever occurs in the course of measurement is expressed in scientifically appropriate terms. This is similar to the use of the less explicit rules and categories that we have discussed already. After discussing scientific measurement, then, we turn to a study of legal decisions, whose rules are also quite explicit, but less so than scientific measurement. Practical reasoning in categorizing can then be discussed with reference to a broad range of settings in which explicit categories and rules of procedure are imposed to various degrees.

OPERATIONAL DEFINITIONS

Scientific measurement is the modern standard for precision in empirical categorization. In recent years philosophers of science have seldom claimed that science is fundamentally different from other measurements. However, claims continue to be made that science is especially precise, reliable, careful, and useful relative to other systems of measurement (Ziman 1978). The precision of scientific measurement is achieved by holding scientific researchers to several procedural requirements. Measurement procedures must be followed precisely. Measurement procedures must be described along with the results, in enough detail so that other researchers can tell from the study how the results were achieved and can replicate the procedures if they want. Data must be recorded and be reported independently of the motives and interests of the researcher. Rigorous training makes it possible for measurement procedures to be followed precisely and described succinctly. The measurement procedures are generally called *operational definitions.*

Uniformity and precision in these procedures is crucial to scientific research. It will help, I think, to consider a contrasting case in which imprecision and variety of measurement procedure are not so important. When I undergo physical examinations, I am weighed by the doctor's staff. There is considerable inconsistency in the weighing procedure from visit to visit. The scale is in a relatively public place. I do not disrobe completely. The staff does not specify whether my shoes should be taken off, or sweaters, or other clothing nonessential to modesty. If I always remain fully dressed, my weight will be influenced by the difference in the weights of my summer and winter clothing. I can also alter my weight by my decision to remove or not remove my shoes and other clothing. The comparisons between my weight at different times, and between my weight and the weight of other patients, cannot be made precisely.

In this situation, the imprecision does not matter much, of course. The doctor makes the important evaluations by looking at me while my clothing is off. But in a research study on the effects of diet or exercise, for instance, in which weight must be determined accurately, this degree of imprecision will not do. To conduct a scientific study, a standardized weighing procedure must be used. To understand the study fully, the reader must know what the procedure was. The reader must know whether the subjects were clothed or not, and, if they were clothed, how the weight of the clothing was controlled. The reader must know how much time passed between the subjects' last meal and weighing and whether wastes passed too. In some studies, the nature and size of the meals may be relevant, as may the exact volumes of liquid and solid wastes. In others, this information may be unnecessary. These procedures define what weight means in the study, and the report of them communicates that meaning to the reader.

Uniformly followed measuring procedures, though, must meet one additional criterion to be scientifically useful. The procedure must be a valid way to perform the desired measurement. In social psychological experiments, for example, part of the measurement procedure is the choosing of subjects for the experiments. Volunteer subjects have been consistently shown to respond differently to experimental situations than have nonvolunteer subjects. An experimenter can choose to solicit volunteers, or can arrange to make participation in the experiment a requirement of some course, or can grant extra course credit for participation but leave the decision to the students. All three ways of gathering subjects are commonly employed, but each one produces slightly different results. Thus, the experimenter cannot validly assume that measurements made on one kind of subject will apply to other kinds of subjects. It has also been suggested that college students, the most frequent human experimental subjects, are not necessarily a valid representation of the entire population. They are more intelligent, on average, and more literate. Their motivations may be different.

The choice of an operational definition, then, limits what one can validly say about the results. Reporting the procedure makes it possible for the reader to judge the validity of the measurements as well as to replicate them. For both uses, it is necessary that the operational definition be completely reported. But the researcher does not report every condition under which the measurements were made. The researcher reports, rather, in sufficient detail to establish the validity and replicability of his or her measurements, and no more. The researcher reports those conditions of the measurement that, according to scientific norms, might influence the results if they were changed. What is necessary to report, then, varies with what is being measured.

Consider the measurement of weight. A sound operational definition of weight must include a description of the clothing worn by the people being weighed. The clothing of the people doing the weighing, though, is irrelevant. There is no indication that the clothing of the people doing the weighing affects the weight of the people being weighed. Thus, information about the weighers' clothing can be omitted from a sound operational definition.

But, even in medical measurements, the clothing of the people performing the measurements is not always irrelevant. Orne and Scheibe (1964) conducted an intriguing experiment. Experimental subjects were subjected to all the trappings of a psychologically dangerous experimental situation—one in which sensory deprivation was induced. They were screened by physical and psychological criteria. They were asked to sign documents that relieved the hospital from liability. They were informed of the dangers of the study. They were exposed to all the trappings of a modern hospital—elaborate instruments, the familiar, forbidding appearance, a staff dressed in medical uniforms and carrying medical regalia. They were not, however, actually subjected to sensory deprivation. Nonetheless, the trappings of the experiment, including the clothing and manner of the experimenters, were enough to induce many of the symptoms of sensory deprivation. The social conditions under which measurement is conducted may be relevant, indeed, to social scientific studies.[2]

Consider the measurement of weight just once more. Suppose that I decided to enlist the subjects as my collaborators in a study of weight and asked them to report their own weights to me. I shall inquire about the type of scale they used and instruct them to report their weight at a particular time of day. However, I will not check their accuracy by means other than those that can be included in the questionnaire. Especially, I will not check their scales or weigh any subjects myself to check their veracity and accuracy. Would you consider the results of this study an accurate measure of weight?

Well, I wouldn't. And, if this seems to belabor something very obvious, consider that much social scientific research is done in precisely this way. The social scientist uses surveys. In the survey, each respondent becomes a collaborator, but one whose accuracy is not checked except by internal design of the questionnaire. Social scientists use official statistics. Whoever gathers and records the statistics becomes a collaborator, whose procedures for recording the statistics are not scrutinized. Social scientists conduct experiments. The interaction between the experimenter and the subjects is seldom reported as part of the experimental situation. But studies show that it affects the results. Social scientists conduct participant observation studies. The words of the subjects must frequently be taken as evidence of unwitnessed events.

Aaron Cicourel (1964; 1968; 1974b) has made this collaboration between researchers and their subjects one of the major topics of his research. He argues that the practical reasoning of any subjects who serve as collaborators in the gathering of data must be included in the operational definitions reported in sociological research. The procedures by which official statistics are gathered, for instance, would become as explicit a part of social scientific research reports as the formalized procedures followed by the researcher.

Cicourel has also been concerned with the reflexivity of scientific accounts. First, he argues that scientific accounts, like others, are embedded in a context that must be known to make them explicit. Second, he argues that social scientific findings about accounts apply to the social scientific accounts as well. If accounts have a characteristic formal structure, then that formal structure must characterize scientific accounts. This implies that practical reasoning should be a self-concealing part of scientific research. Thus, the study of scientific measurement is a critical test of ethnomethodological assertions. It also implies that the practical reasoning of the researcher as he or she conducts the research ought to be recorded and reported as part of the methodology of the study. Cicourel's

---

[2] There is extensive evidence that the experimental setting influences the results of psychological experiments. Aronson and Carlsmith (1968) review the literature. Wuebben, Straits, and Schulman (1974) and Miller (1972) collected several studies and include good lists of references.

work recommends extensive changes in the way in which social scientific research is reported. He identifies an extensive range of matters that affect the results of studies and that are necessary to understand fully but are not now included in research reports.

I have suggested that scientific accounts are reflexive in the sense that, when they concern accounts, they apply to themselves. This assertion is less obvious than it may appear. In fact, it is only true of scientific statements because of the special standards that scientists set for themselves. It is not necessarily true of commonsense accounts about accounts.

Commonsense accounts cannot be taken literally. There is considerable folk wisdom, for example, that people drink alcohol to avoid facing their problems. People drink to forget or to run away from their troubles. People hide in the bottle. They drown their sorrows. Taken literally, these statements should also apply to whoever makes the statement if that person drinks alcohol. But in practical situations, it does not. The unqualified term "people" is not intended as unqualified. Especially, the speaker is not accountably admitting that he or she is trying to avoid problems by drinking. Accounts such as those concerning the meaning of drinking may appear reflexive in the sense that they apply to the person making them, but they are not. The literal interpretation of the words as unqualified is not appropriate.

Warriner (1973) observed an informative contrast between the public and private uses of alcohol and the publicly and privately expressed attitudes about drinking in a "dry," rural community. A public morality held that drinking alcohol was immoral and that only "bums and other elements of the lower classes drank" (Warriner 1973, p. 50). Extensive observation disclosed no public violation or rejection of this moral stance. At home, however, and in the company of friends, moderate alcohol drinking was regularly observed. Even some members of the Women's Christian Temperance Union served alcohol in such settings. Despite publicly supporting the public morality of the community, many people, in private, said that moderate alcohol use was not immoral. Some recognized the inconsistency and concluded that the town was full of hypocrites who "vote dry and drink wet" (Warriner 1973, p. 51).

Several reasons were given for the inconsistency between public and private conduct. Some wanted to avoid arguments and said that others would just give a big fight if you contradicted the public morality. Some explicitly said that they could handle alcohol and drink moderately but that others could not and must be shielded from temptation. But the people who wanted to avoid fights also expressed the same views as the people they thought would harrass them for expressing their private views. There is no indication that people included themselves among the hypocrites for concealing their drinking. In short, a variety of opinions was expressed that could not be taken literally to apply to the person who made them, even when that person acted like those about whom he or she was talking.

However, literal interpretations of scientific interpretations are appropriate. Scientists claim for themselves a level of precision that supports taking empirical statements at face value. Even if the looseness of empirical terms is recognized, claims are made that scientific use deserves extreme confidence. Therefore, any scientific statement about accounts applies to itself, since it is an account too. The importance of this kind of reflexivity is relative to the content of the statements about accounts. Many social scientists have described human reasoning as a correctible approximation of traditional logic.[3] The reflexivity of that statement about human reasoning has no interesting methodological implications. Human reasoning may be mistaken or ill informed, but it has the same formal characteristics as the formal systems used in scientific theory. Scientists avoid the worst errors by training and attention to precision. The public can be educated.

But when the statement about accounts is that they display a formal structure different from traditional logic, the implications are much different. Science must be redefined. If scientists do not want this statement to be taken literally, they must forego claims to relatively great rigor and precision. If they accept the statement as reflexively true about science, they must concede the influence of practical reasoning and interests in measurement and the looseness of their terms. Whether this statement is accepted literally by scientists or not, then, the claims of science must be redefined. Thus, the accuracy of the statement, empirically, is very important. And, for the reasons outlined earlier, this issue is more relevant in the social sciences than in the more precise physical sciences. Social scientists do not have the luxury of claiming that their work is so precise that formal challenges are irrelevant. The contentious response to ethnomethodology results, in large part, from its implication that science is not being done or reported properly by social scientists.

STUDYING PRACTICAL REASONING
IN SOCIAL SCIENTIFIC MEASUREMENT

Cicourel (1968; 1974a) developed an ingenious way to study the intrusion of practical reasoning into scientific measurement procedures that are designed to exclude them. To study this topic, a scientific study that is accepted as competent by the scientific community must provide the data. The issue is not whether scientists engage in practical reasoning but only whether they do so while they are conducting proper scientific measurement. But the elimination, or at least extreme reduction, of commonsense thought in science is a sanctioned norm of the scientific community. To have one's research investigated and shown to in-

---

[3]   See Wilson (1970) for a well-documented discussion of this view, which he incorporates in his model of the "normative paradigm." Wilson argues that this view of reasoning is the dominant one in sociology.

clude commonsense reasoning where scientific methodology should prevail is to have one's competence as a scientist called into question. The ethnomethodological view that everyone engages in practical reasoning at all times, that it cannot be excluded, and that it is not blameworthy is of little comfort. And it will offer little comfort to the scientist until the sanctioned norms of the scientific community change to recognize this argument. Thus, it is unlikely that practicing scientists will welcome the role of subject in this sort of ethnomethodological study. This is one of the limits placed on accountable research topics by the norms of the scientific community.

Cicourel has contrived to overcome this normative resistance by conducting his own studies and simultaneously recording the practical reasoning that is ordinarily omitted from social scientific reports. This is a difficult program to follow. It requires the interest and expertise to conduct scientifically competent studies, using the standard research methods recognized in the social scientific community in an accountable way. At the same time, it requires an interest in practical reasoning and the competence to recognize and record the relevant data to study it

This dual program gives Cicourel's studies a complex and peculiar character. On the one hand, he includes conventional sociological research reports. This is essential to establish that the study he has conducted is a competent one and therefore reflects on the practice of competent science. On the other hand, he includes his ethnomethodological study of the practical reasoning that contributed to the conventional study. The description of the practical reasoning is not criticism of his own study. The conventional study is presented as competent. Rather, judgment is suspended about how the reasoning is actually done, and the actual reasoning is described, whether it fits normative conceptions of science or not. The logistics of presenting these two types of material in an easily readable form are not fully worked out. Cicourel's own studies, that include reports of practical reasoning as a topic, serve as a working model for how social research ought to be reported.

An example of this blend of concerns was discussed in the first chapter and bears reconsideration in this context. Cicourel reported that, in studying the processing of juvenile cases, he was unable to attend all the official hearings. As a result, his information on each case was a composite of hearsay, direct observation, and official reports. In addition, the official files on each case were partial and cryptic. That is, they were bad records in the same ways as were those encountered by Garfinkel in the medical clinic. Cicourel interpreted those files using his own knowledge of the case and of typical procedures and also discussed them with the officials involved. They provided information on what the files meant and why they were recorded as they were. Here, again, hearsay becomes crucial to the study and, in addition, Cicourel's own implicit knowledge of the setting informs the results. To fully understand his cases, Cicourel was compelled to approach files in the very way coders could not. We see, then, that the practical interests of Cicourel's subjects, his own practical, logistic problems in studying the cases, and his own accumulated implicit knowledge of the settings are all instrumental in his final description of the cases.

The most remarkable thing about the hodgepodge character of ethnographic data is that it is seldom reported. Cicourel has consistently argued that it ought to be recorded because the sense of what we know about juvenile cases is transformed by including these facts about the studies. The very fact that it changes the meaning of the final report to include this information about how the facts were gathered is grounds for revising scientific practice to routinely include it. The norms that exclude reports of the intrusion of practical reasoning and require that the research be reported in terms of normative scientific standards are shown to conceal the operation of practical reasoning. In this respect, they are like the other norms we have considered.

Juvenile Justice: Some Effects of Practical Reasoning on Official Standards

In the course of his study of the administration of juvenile justice in two communities, Cicourel (1968) maintained detailed records of the disposition of cases. These records allowed him to study how the official disposition of cases, and the records they created, are influenced by the practical circumstances of the case. He found, for example, that the marital situation of the juvenile offender's parents influenced whether and how offenses would be officially recorded. That is, the same type of offense might be recorded in various ways, depending on the juvenile's family situation. The officials in both communities subscribed to the commonsense assumption that broken homes cause juvenile delinquency. As a result, offenses committed by juveniles from broken homes, homes in which the parents were not both present, were considered more serious than were the same offenses committed by a juvenile in an intact family. In the former case, the offense was a sign that the juvenile, without a proper family to guide him or her, had begun to show signs of delinquency. These signs were expected to increase, and action was taken to try to prevent serious trouble by using the official legal machinery. In the latter case, the offense was regarded as less serious because the intact family was a resource that could help straighten out the offender before his or her actions became too serious. The official legal machinery was not employed (Cicourel 1968, pp. 36-37).

The result of this practical reasoning about the effects of the family situation on juveniles was to systematically treat juveniles from broken homes differently from juveniles from intact homes. Offenses committed by juveniles from broken homes were officially recorded more frequently, and the legal machinery was more often involved in resolving their problems. As a result, juveniles from broken homes had greater official records of delinquency than did juveniles from intact homes who committed similar offenses. Thus, the practice of anticipating the effects of the broken home on the juveniles' later conduct was to create statistics that supported the original assumptions involved. Further, official records of delinquency may well have limited the educational and career options of the juveniles. The effect of those limitations should be to have the children from intact families straighten out, overcome their early unrecorded offenses, and become exemplary adults more often than the juveniles from broken homes. Thus, official records, by limiting options, would create results that justified the original judgment that the juveniles from broken homes were beginning a predictable sequence of serious and consequential delinquency.

These practical arrangements make official statistics invalid measures for many scientific questions. They do not reveal the true incidence of offenses or their true nature. They cannot be used to compare rates of delinquency among different types of juveniles. For example, rates of delinquency among juveniles from broken homes cannot validly be compared with rates of delinquency among juveniles from intact families. In general, whenever assumptions about groups of juveniles influence the ways in which their offenses are recorded and settled, the official records do not validly reflect the conduct of those groups. In addition, the records serve to provide evidence for the assumptions that guided their creation. The importance of the assumptions, then, is self-concealing. Most important, the assumptions are a self-concealing procedure in any scientific study based on official statistics as well as in the everyday life of the community.

Comparison of activities in two communities disclosed differences between the ways in which juvenile offenses were processed. In one of the communities the mayor intervened periodically in the day-to-day activities of the police department. His intervention was primarily to convey political influence and family pressures through his office to the juvenile authorities. The result of this intervention was that influence with the mayor, whether through political affiliation or through family standing in the community, could be easily brought to bear on the disposition of juvenile cases. The official records should reflect this procedure. Cases were not handled formally, in court, unless adverse publicity made that politically expedient.

In the other community, the administrative officer was a city-manager, not a mayor, and the administrative arrangement was less political. The police department in that community maintained a more professional orientation in juvenile cases and was less subject to political influence. The city-manager would not intervene in day-to-day police activities, and the police department was sufficiently politically independent to preclude direct interference. In accord with their more professional orientation, the police utilized the courts and probation system more regularly. Use of the courts and other formal mechanisms, of course, generated more juveniles with official recorded offenses.

In this comparison we can see that official legal records are reflexive accounts that must be understood in the context of the activities of the communities and legal systems that create them. Any study that utilizes the statistics shares in that reflexivity and can only be made clear by including the activities involved in creating the records in the description of how the study was conducted. A general understanding of the practical reasoning involved will not suffice. To understand the statistics, we must know how the people in each particular community and legal system respond to offenses, record them, and dispose of the cases. Since these activities influence the results of the studies, an account of them is relevant to operational definitions. More generally, the participation of untrained people as collaborators in the gathering of research must be more fully acknowledged.

Argentine Fertility: Practical Reasoning of the Trained Research Staff

The intrusion of practical reasoning in Cicourel's study of the administration of juvenile justice had two major sources. First, the use of official records and files amounted to enlisting untrained individuals who were pursuing their own practical ends, not the goal of scientific validity, as collaborators in the research. In effect, the practical decision-making of the legal system was incorporated into the research. Second, Cicourel encountered logistic problems in trying to observe events firsthand. Schedule conflicts occurred which made it necessary for him to rely on a mixture of personal observation, official files, and hearsay as evidence of the processing of cases. This enlisted additional collaborators and, in addition, forced Cicourel to make practical judgments about which events were more important, whose word he could trust, how to interpret official records, and so on.

It might be possible to eliminate these two sources of practical reasoning in social scientific research. First, the subjects of the study could be used as subjects only, not as collaborators. Their activities could be observed firsthand, and their own reports could be accepted only in a scientifically acceptable form such as questionnaires. The logistic problems could be solved by utilizing a research team of trained observers. Thus, one researcher would still be unable to observe all events firsthand, but only the reports of trained observers, committed to valid research, would be used. In his study of Argentine fertility, Cicourel (1974a) showed that practical reasoning must be employed, even when the data are collected by a trained research team.

Cicourel's study of fertility was based on a preformulated questionnaire. In addition to the questions, probes were required to elicit more detail and encourage more complete answers. As in all studies of this type, the interviewer must assess the answers of the subject and decide whether they are complete and whether a probe will gather more information or offend the subject. Thus, the interviewers were routinely involved in practical judgments of the rapport between the subjects and themselves. This estimate affected the gathering of data.

Questions raised in studies of fertility covered several highly personal matters and the possibility of offending the subjects was considerable. The reluctance of subjects to talk openly on these subjects was also a factor in the research. The study of fertility required data on intended family size, frequency of sexual intercourse, sexual practices, and the use of contraceptives. The questions about such matters as contraception and family planning were especially touchy in a predominantly Catholic country such as Argentina. The importance of frequent intercourse to the self-images of pride of the subjects may also have been variable.

The personal and emotional character of these topics made the relationship between the interviewer and the subjects even more important to receiving frank answers. Ordinarily, interviewers were reluctant to admit that they could not establish rapport with their subjects because it reflected on their competence. But Cicourel encouraged them to report when interviews did not seem to be proceeding well.[4]

Cicourel divided his interview into two sections. One section contained relatively impersonal, demographic questions. The second section included the more personal questions. By not reducing pay for uncompleted interviews and by making it routine for the second half of the interview to be conducted by a different interviewer, Cicourel reduced the threat of failed rapport to his staff. Staff members who felt that they could not get frank answers to the personal questions terminated the session, reported their impressions of the subject, and participated in the attempt to find an interviewer on the staff who seemed better matched to the subject.

From the reports, a typology of subjects emerged. At one extreme, some subjects refused to even be interviewed. At the other, some subjects answered even the most personal questions in great detail and, in the opinion of the interviewers, honestly and fully. The judgment of rapport is problematic. Cicourel (1974a, p. 86) reported, for example, that some refusals to be interviewed were preceded by "as much as three hours of discussion, wine drinking, and friendly conversation" with the interviewer. How that judgment was made, then, whether for the purpose of using probes or for the purpose of matching interviewers to subjects for personal questions, is a relevant topic in the operational definition of questionnaire items.

Whenever questionnaires are used, the honesty and accuracy of the answers to questions is essential to the validity of the results. When probes are employed, the interviewer must make a series of practical judgments. The interviewer must decide when the subjects must be pressed to answer more fully and when they must be left alone. Practical considerations of pay and

---

[4]   This did not require the interviewers to make judgments any different from those involved in using probes. Those judgments were reported, though, and were put to a different purpose. There is the chance, of course, that Cicourel's encouragement created a record of rapport problems in the same way that police assumptions create a record of greater juvenile delinquency in broken families.

professional competence discouraged interviewers from acknowledging their inability to get satisfactory answers from particular subjects. When these discouraging factors were reduced, however, interviewers reported that they often did not establish rapport with subjects. They did not feel that the subjects would respond honestly and fully. The judgment was a practical one, and problematic. However, the trained interviewer was routinely required to make the judgment by questionnaires using probes. In studies that do not gather the information about rapport, there is the possibility that the data are not honest and complete. We are led, then, to these conclusions. The relationship between the subject and the interviewer appears to affect the answers to interview questions.[5] The way in which probes are employed seems to be relevant to the operational definition of data. Interviewers' assessments of rapport need further examination to determine whether they have an influence on results.

A second problem addressed by Cicourel was the ability of the subjects to understand questions. Questionnaire items, it must be remembered, were posed to people from diverse socioeconomic, ethnic, religious, and educational backgrounds. The same words could not be assumed to be comprehended alike by these various types of people. But if the questions had different meanings for different subjects, what did the answers mean? Would it be proper to tabulate them as answers to the same question?

Cicourel argues that the practice of treating responses to questionnaires as answers to the same questions is not justified. The issue is whether to standardize the words used in the question or the subjects' understandings of it. In most studies that employ questionnaires, the interviewers are discouraged from explaining the questions to the subjects. They can repeat the question, but they are discouraged from rephrasing it. This approach standardizes what each subject hears. However, in such studies, the interviewers frequently felt impelled to explain the question. But no procedure is provided in the research to determine how often this occurs, how the interviewer manages the task, and how he or she decides that the subject understands (Cicourel 1974a, p. 89). Thus, despite efforts to standardize the words said to subjects, interviewers explain the questions in idiosyncratic ways and to an unknown extent. That is, the desired type of standardization is not achieved. And, once this practice is recognized to occur, the question arises of whether the subjects understand the questions they answer. Even the use of machines to standardize the spoken words would not settle that issue. In effect, this form of standardization, by creating data in precoded forms and not reporting information about the comprehension of subjects or the exceptions made by researchers, conceals the evidence necessary to evaluate the assumption that all is well.

[5]   An experiment by Rosenfeld and Baer (1969) indicates how difficult it is for interviewers to evaluate this relationship. In it, an interviewer was misled about what his subject knew and was manipulated by him.

Cicourel argues that the meaning, rather than the wording, of the question must be standardized. He encouraged his interviewers to use their judgment and explain questions when necessary. They were also instructed to record the fact that an explanation was necessary, but Cicourel did not report the frequency of explanations. On this point, Cicourel's research is only suggestive. The degree to which the wording of questions is actually standardized is concealed by the way in which the data were reported. Some evidence exists that subjects did not always understand the questions, but we cannot be sure that this introduces a bias into the results. Once again, the relationship between the interviewer and the subject was suggested as a topic that ought to be investigated as part of the methodology of the social sciences and addressed in its operational definitions. In addition, the ways in which questions were explained and the comprehension of the subjects established appear relevant. Practical reasoning was apparently involved in the practices of trained interviewers, but the impact of this on results can only be determined empirically.

THE PRACTICAL USE OF SCIENTIFIC RESULTS

One important instance of the application of scientific findings in practical decision making has been studied by ethnomethodologists. That instance is the use of standardized tests in public schools, especially to sort graduates of kindergarten into different first-grade classes. The separation of students into different curriculum groups is both consequential for the child and controversial. The effects on the child are of two types. First, the decision enters the child's permanent records and, whether favorably or unfavorably, may influence later decisions based on those records. Second, the exposure of the child to a particular curriculum tends to make movement to a different group increasingly difficult as time passes. The child who might have been able to do the work in a given program from the start may not be able to catch up after being in a slower group for a lengthy period. In any event, the transition becomes harder and harder as time passes.

The controversy over this "tracking" of students centers on the wisdom of separating students and also on the accuracy of the procedures by which they are separated. Even among those who favor tracking, the question of how to judge the students' abilities remains. Standardized testing is a frequent sorting tool. The tests claim several merits. They are scientifically designed by experts. They generate scores that compare each child with a large, national sample. They replace the judgment of the classroom teacher, which is often regarded as too subjective for such an important matter. In short, the tests are scientific.

Leiter (1974; 1976) conducted a study of the use of standardized test results in making concrete decisions about the placement of children in first-grade classes. But Leiter (1976) found that the test results were not used mechanically, by a predetermined formula, to assign students to an appropriate first-grade class. Instead, the scores were incorporated into a decision process that also utilized other information available to the kindergarten teachers who made the decisions. For example, one girl scored in the average group with respect to learning rates, but quite low with respect to the recognition of phonemes. Her difficulty with phonemes depressed overall scores considerably. The teacher attributed the lowered score to the fact that the girl was Spanish speaking. Her experience at home did not provide practice in the use of English phonemes. The teacher added, too, her classroom knowledge that the girl had an excellent attention span and motivation level. Her conclusion was that the girl should be placed in a junior first grade to work on her specific problem, but with the specific recommendation that she be considered for movement to a regular first-grade class if her reading was not hampered by her difficulty with sounds. In the assembling of the teacher's classroom knowledge, impressions of the child, and estimates of why the scores on the test were low, it is clear that the practical, subjective reasoning of the teacher was not replaced by the use of tests. Rather, the tests were incorporated into that reasoning process.

This background information can be used in more striking ways. After all, in the case I just discussed, the girl was assigned to a class that was appropriate given her test scores. The teacher's knowledge was utilized only to alert the first-grade teacher to facts that might make the test misleading and to reconsider the child's case during the school year. However, because of background information known to the teacher, students with better scores on the standardized tests may be sent to a junior first grade whereas those with lower scores are sent to a regular first grade. In one such case, the student with lower test scores was said to have good work habits. In addition, the teacher thought he was brighter than the tests showed and she mistrusted the low score in his case. The teacher speculated that he was under pressure (from his parents) to achieve and simply became confused during the test. All these impressions and speculations, as well as the test scores, informed the placement of the child.

The student who scored better on the test was understood to be academically, but not emotionally, prepared for first grade. The teacher perceived his attention span as being too brief. During the test, the teacher recalled, she had to work to keep his attention. Immaturity and emotional problems combined to make him unready to sit still and pay attention long enough to learn reading. He was assigned to a junior first grade with a recommendation to the first-grade teacher that she consider referring him for counseling.

Thus, the test, whose virtues are connected to its objectivity and its replacement of subjective teacher evaluations, was used by incorporation into teachers' evaluations. The scores were not used rigidly, nor in isolation. They were interpreted in the context of other knowledge the teacher had of the child. In placing the child, the teacher considered the test scores, her impressions of the child's attention span, of the child's ability to sit still and not disrupt a reading group, and of the child's personality and ability to work independently while the teacher was working with others (Leiter 1974). In addition, the teacher acknowledged a bureaucratic imperative: the existence of a junior first grade and facilities for it required that some students be placed there. Thus, in part, the placement of students was a judgment of each case on its merits. And, in part, the process was one of sorting, with rough guidelines for the numbers to be assigned to each class set in advance.

We can conclude, then, that the use of standardized tests has not replaced practical reasoning or subjective teachers' judgments. Instead, the tests are used as a diagnostic tool and are incorporated into the selection processes that they were meant to replace. The use of scientific results, then, in the making of practical decisions does not generate exceptions to the invariant presence of practical decision making.

COMMON SENSE AS A MODEL FOR SCIENCE; SCIENCE AS A MODEL FOR COMMON SENSE

The ethnomethodological studies of science suggest that our understanding of practical reasoning applies to scientific research. Normative and political concerns in the scientific and larger communities influence what scientists study, how they study it, and what they consider accountable scientific research methods and reports. In the social sciences, the actual measurement procedures can easily be shown to include practical reasoning. Whatever practical reasoning the subjects engage in is part of the method by which the data are gathered. Second, the researchers themselves must make practical decisions that affect the results of their studies. Some are simple logistic decisions. Others involve ongoing judgment of whether the questions have been understood by the subject, whether the subject is answering truthfully, and whether the setting of the research tends to impose answers on subjects without their awareness.

Operational definition is the common term for a description of how a term is properly used and measurements properly made in science. Operational definitions in the social sciences would profit, apparently, by expansion to include practical reasoning. When scientific results are employed in practical decision-making, they enter the decision process as evidence that is used along with other evidence and in the same way. Despite the imposition of exacting rules of procedure and relatively greater precision in the application of procedures, science remains a commonsense activity. Commonsense reasoning is not replaced. Other standards are added to it.

Because science is a commonsense activity, we could use our knowledge of commonsense reasoning as a model of science. The point of using models at all is to exploit greater knowledge or some other advantage of investigating in one area to gain insight in another. For example, performance testing a plane in a wind tunnel is a model of building and flying a real plane. It is cheaper. It is easier to make measurements. People are not aboard if things don't work out right. It doesn't sound sensible to use an actual plane to give insight into the performance of mock-ups in wind tunnels. Still, engineers do it. After the wind tunnel has been used as a model for actual flight, the actual flight is tried and measurements are taken. The results anticipated on the basis of wind tunnel tests are compared with what actually happens. The wind tunnel, which is used to improve plane design, is itself improved by considering the plane as a model for its model.

Our understanding of practical reasoning has been used as a model of science. We were aware that science utilizes an extensive set of explicit rules and formal arguments. We were also aware that commonsense reasoning is self-concealing and might be significant in the practice of science without being noticed. Our philosophical reasoning suggested that commonsense reasoning must be employed in science in the placement of events into loose categories by measurement and in the judgment that steps in explicit formal arguments are valid. But the philosophical reasoning does not specify whether the presence of commonsense reasoning is important, that is, whether it operates in a way that should reduce our confidence in scientific measurement and our willingness to use scientific results as if they were stated in well-defined categories. We still do not know how important the commonsense component of scientific reasoning and measurement is. Some studies suggest that commonsense reasoning is easily demonstrable in the social sciences, but a procedure has not yet been employed to determine the extent to which the precision of scientific measurement and reasoning are compromised by commonsense reasoning. We can be fairly certain that claims of science replacing commonsense procedures are false. Apparently, scientific standards and procedures are imposed upon commonsense standards and procedures and the two coexist in approximately the way our philosophical reasoning led us to expect. This suggests that the scientific claims to be more precise than commonsense must be empirically investigated. Finally, in the social sciences, if not the natural sciences, some expansion of the topics to be included in operational definitions seems warranted. I believe that this expansion has begun in the years since these arguments were first raised by ethnomethodologists and others. But there is still no systematic evidence concerning its importance or its effects on precision.

Our knowledge of science can also enlighten our knowledge of practical sense if we use it as a model. First, we know that scientists are exceptionally careful in their observations and inferences. They do not feel that accounts can be properly understood unless operational definitions are included. That is, they want to know the procedures used to arrive at observations and inferences. Using science as a model for common sense, then, leads to the conclusion that, to understand commonsense reasoning, one must be able to define the terms and processes operationally, in terms of actual practices and procedures. Thus, there is no necessary departure from scientific method in ethnomethodology, which, for other reasons, is already interested in such definitions.[6]

Second, considering the way in which commonsense reasoning is employed in science is instructive for ethnomethodological study. We have seen, sketchily, that there is no contradiction between improving precision and imposing additional explicit standards of observation and reasoning and the continued presence of common sense. Thus, the recognition that common sense is invariantly employed in sense-making does not in any way imply that our studies of sense-making cannot be made more precise, cannot legitimately be held to additional standards of reasoning, and cannot become scientific. All that the invariance of common sense does imply in this connection is that no matter how careful we become, no matter what standards we impose upon ourselves, it will always be possible to find the operation of commonsense reasoning in our activities. However, after precision and adherence to the explicit additional standards reach sufficiently high levels, the commonsense component becomes irrelevant for all practical purposes except the better understanding of how common sense works.

OPERATIONAL DEFINITIONS IN ORGANIZATIONAL SETTINGS

I should like to exploit our use of scientific methodology as a model for commonsense activities by considering an example of what is involved, operationally, in the use of terms in an organizational setting. We shall see that participation in bureaucratic activities imposes rules and other contingencies on commonsense reasoning. Decisions in the bureaucracy reflect these imposed rules, priorities among goals, practical contingencies, and the pattern of routine activities that are involved in the use of bureaucratic categories. All these matters are essential to an operational definition of the terms used in the bureaucracy.

Police Apprehension of the Mentally Ill

Bittner (1967b) studied the standardized activities that contributed to police judgments that a person should be categorized as mentally ill, apprehended, and taken to a psychiatric hospital. Police usually had to make this determination after having been called to the scene by family members, neighbors, or

---

[6] Cicourel refers to these operational definitions as interpretive procedures. Practical reasoning, members' methods, members' practices, the documentary method, and other terms are also used for them.

others who had already decided that something official needed to be done. Thus, there was reduced resistance to apprehension and removal of the person from his or her family and others present. Still, the police were reluctant to remove the person and begin proceedings leading to psychiatric commitment. This was a course of last resort, a category that the police resisted using. A description of what this categorization meant, operationally, will indicate why this reluctance existed.

First, the police had their own careers to consider. The bureaucratic rewards were most generous for making arrests and for other involvements in crime control. The skills involved in controlling family disputes or apprehending the mentally ill were not especially rewarded by superiors. Thus, to invest time in such pursuits, even if one demonstrated extraordinary skill, was not good professional police practice. Operationally, activities involving family disputes and potential psychiatric commitment were relative wastes of time. The time would have been better spent, from the standpoint of advancing one's career, in crime control, especially in making arrests. One wanted to handle family disputes, bizarre behavior, psychotic episodes, and the like as quickly as possible.

If an officer decided that a person was an appropriate candidate for psychiatric examination or commitment, the proper course was to take that person to a psychiatric hospital. If the officer were to do so, however, he or she would lose control over the case to a considerable extent. First, the officer must comply with hospital procedure, including time-consuming paperwork and simple waiting. His or her initial judgment that the person was mentally ill may be contradicted by the doctors who make the examination. The officer would then be stuck with an aggravated problem. The person must be taken back to the setting from which he or she was removed and that situation must be dealt with again in a new way. Thus, to categorize a person as mentally ill committed one to a time-consuming and poorly rewarded procedure, at best. At worst, it exacerbated the problem and required still more time to resettle the situation. The lengthiness of the proceedings and their uncertain outcome created the possibility of failure to conclude the case in a reasonable time. Bringing cases to closure is another very important criterion by which police are judged.

Thus, even when a person appeared to be mentally ill to the police and a potential source of future trouble, the police were reluctant to categorize him or her as such and proceed on that basis. Suicide attempts would likely lead to apprehension. The inability of family or friends to cope with the behavior encouraged apprehension. Disturbance of normal physical appearance—nudity, incontinence, extreme dirtiness, and so on—were also frequent grounds for apprehension. Extreme agitation, especially when there was some threat of violence, was another. So was serious disorientation.

What does it mean, then, for a person to be apprehended as mentally ill by the police and taken to the psychiatric hospital for examination or commitment? There is a legal definition that states when a person can be treated in that way.

There are typical symptoms and situations that reliably indicate that the police will treat the person as mentally ill. And, most important, there are a variety of contingencies of what the category of mental illness means, operationally, to the people who use it. It means a risk of time wasted in bad police work. It means surrendering control of the case to doctors and to hospital bureaucracies. It means engaging in activities that, even if done well, would not result in bureaucratic rewards. These practices, and others surrounding the use of categories, are part of their meaning and part of the reasoning that governs their use. The police bureaucracy made a variety of categories available to the officer, many of which could be used to describe and govern that officer's activities. The procedures that were involved with the various categories were influential in the choice among them. Thus, it mattered, procedurally, what a thing was called when there were choices available. Placing events in different categories involved one in different courses of actions, different procedures. These are part of the operational definitions of terms in actual use. As Robert Frost put it, "all the fun's in how you say a thing."

The practical considerations of the police officer in making this judgment were primarily oriented to the consequences of the use of different categories. People look to the future, assuming that what they have learned from the past will apply once again.[7] We orient ourselves to expected future events. But, if we want to fully understand the decision, we will have to consider prior operations as well—operations that lead up to the decision. How does a person come to be called a police officer? How do police officers come to have the normative right to make this judgment? How do police officers come to have the view of the future that they do? Ethnomethodologists argue that, if we enumerate these operations completely, we will find that there is no more to social organization. Social organization consists entirely of the practices (or methods, or procedures, or operations, or strategies, or behavior) by which it is made accountable.

SUMMARY

The rules governing scientific research and reports are not a replacement for practical reasoning, but are added to it. Practical reasoning is an integral and unavoidable part of the practice of science. This is easily demonstrated in the social sciences. The presence of commonsense reasoning does not imply that science is no more precise than other sense-making activities. Formally, its terms are indexical or loose, but indexical or loose terms are variably precise. Whether they are precise enough or not depends on the uses to which they will be put.

---

[7]   This way of considering the future as an extension of the past, allowing for exceptions, of course, is called retrospective-prospective analysis.

It is clear, I think, that for the goal of creating a sound social science, practical reasoning must be included both as a theoretical topic and as an addition to the methodological communication among researchers. We must understand how people reason, and we must include practical reasoning in operational definitions. Thus, ethnomethodology does offer suggestions for how social science can make improvements. But, in addition, ethnomethodological studies imply that science, or any human activity, will never match the ideal of its own explicit formulations. Implicit practical reasoning will always be present. This does not imply, however, that the degree of precision imposed over commonsense reasoning will not be great enough to support the use of explicit formal systems satisfactorily for the purposes at hand. For example, the presence of commonsense reasoning in medicine does not imply that medicines will not work, that surgery cannot be done, and so on. For those purposes, common sense may not intrude upon the formal reasoning enough to matter. For the purpose of social scientific theory, however, commonsense reasoning will probably remain perpetually interesting.

Finally, we can borrow a little from the formal scientific method in our understanding of practical reasoning. The calculation of interests and the accommodation of plans to practical contingencies appears to be the practical equivalent of using operational definitions. The concern with what events mean and what should be done includes a large interest in what the person will have to do and what will happen as a result of his or her choices. These procedures and events, these operations surrounding the use of categories, are essential to understanding them, whether as a scientist or lay person. They are ethnomethodology's central concern.

Normative and practical considerations limit the categories[8] into which events can be placed. The scientific community regulates what will and will not be reported, of those things that occur. Bureaucratic rules include categories into which events must be placed and, in addition, practical contingencies of life in the bureaucracy regulate still further what will be recorded and how. Subcultures, such as that of illegal drug users, provide vocabularies for their members. Our individual vocabularies are limited samples of the collective vocabulary provided by the English language.

Part of our concern when matching events to categories is the nature of the events themselves. But, in addition, we are concerned with the consequences of using the different alternatives available to us. The use of different categories involves us in different practical outcomes. Different categories are defended differently to those who may hold us accountable. The choice among different applicable categories has consequences for all involved. Practical estimates of these results are based on our practical knowledge of those categories. These

---

[8]   Categorizing events includes perceiving them as instances of a category and reporting a categorization to others. The two categories involved may, of course, be different.

considerations of the uses to which the terms are put and the results of using them are the practical equivalent of operational definitions in scientific categorizing. To understand the use of categories, reasoning with them, and the meaning of events in everyday life, we must define the procedures and operations involved in their use. We must define them operationally, in terms of the practices in which people become involved when different terms are chosen, different plans are activated, and different courses of action are undertaken.

SUGGESTED READINGS

Cicourel (1964) discusses the theoretical issues to which his studies are addressed in detail. Churchill (1971) relates the questions raised by ethnomethodologists about scientific measurement to the possible future contributions of ethnomethodology to scientific measurement procedures. Cicourel and Kitsuse (1963) study the categorization of children in the bureaucratic context of the school. Melbin (1969) documents a fascinating effect of psychiatrist-patient relationships upon behavior. His argument extends the one advanced by Orne and others.

Ethnomethodology is a relatively new specialty, but it is already accepted calmly in the sociology community. It is difficult to appreciate, sometimes, that ethnomethodology and its view of science were angrily received only a few years ago. I heartily recommend looking over the following sample of responses to ethnomethodology. Many of them are book reviews and only a page or so long. McLeod (1975) is short, well done, and bitterly derisive. It should be read by those who have also read Garfinkel and Sacks (1970). The following suggestions do not exhaust the response to ethnomethodology, and I have not included many of the replies (Coser 1975; Denzin 1970; Lennon 1973; Luckman 1972; Mayrl 1973; Rock 1968; Swanson, Wallace, and Coleman 1968; Tiryakian 1974; Touhey 1973; Wilkins 1968; Zimmerman and Wieder 1970).

Watson (1969) gives a fascinating firsthand account of the political activity attending the discovery of the double helix structure of DNA. For those who are disquieted by the qualifications imposed on scientific knowledge, Mead (1964) presents an interesting discussion of what we can accept as true.

6

Conversation Analysis

THE STANDPOINT OF CONVERSATION ANALYSIS

Conversation analysis is a distinctive approach to research within ethnomethodology. Conversation analysts study the social organization of talk by practices contained in the talk itself. The reflexivity of conversation, as embodied in its self-organizing practices, is the core topic of the research. Conversation analysis culminates in the specification of rules to which conversations and conversationalists are held normatively accountable. The rules are understood to be a necessary component of an adequate model of the actor. The rules are relatively independent of the specific topics of conversation. Many apply invariantly in conversation on any topic. Thus, the structure provided by the rules is a formal structure. The rules, though, are indexical in their application. Whether the rules have been adequately followed is a practical judgment made in and for practical situations. The formal structure of practical reasoning applies. In all important respects, then, conversation analysis is conceptually ethnomethodological. The state of conversation is conceived as a social situation. Its organization is studied operationally and with the same concerns that ethnomethodologists bring to the study of other situations. The distinctiveness of conversation analysis lies in its research strategy.

Ethnomethodological studies have typically reflected three principles of abstraction in the selection and bounding of topics. First, each study has selected either a single person or a relatively small collection of people for study. When a collection of people has been studied, those people have not only shared occupancy of a particular social role or interlocking set of roles but have also participated in those roles together. For example, Cicourel's (1974a) study of interviewers working on demographic studies concerned researchers who were part of the same research team rather than, for instance, a sample of researchers working on different projects throughout the United States. Second, the studies have typically been concerned with activities in a geographically and socially defined setting. Hospital clinic workers were not followed home, or observed during off-duty recreation, or studied in all aspects of their lives. Rather, they were selected for study as holders of a particular role and studied only in the clinic, the primary place in which the role was enacted. Third, the studies have typically explored only one, or a very few, substantive themes in the activities of the subjects. We have considerable information concerning how Agnes managed her gender identity but none about her skills as a typist, how she and her roommate divided the household chores, or how successfully she budgeted her income. We know about the social organization of paranoia as a theme in the drug-using community, but we do not know the mating etiquette of that community, whether they read books, or how seriously they pursued their studies. The abstraction of one theme from the complexity of everyday life allows the practices that organize that theme to be studied in detail.

These characteristic modes of abstraction give the empirical portion of ethnomethodological studies a distinctive character. First, they tend to be detailed studies of narrowly delimited aspects of social life. They seldom attempt to capture the life of a group or community as a whole. Second, themes other than the main topic enter the studies as practical contingencies of organizing the selected theme. For example, the conditions imposed by the social organization of physical examinations enter the study of Agnes only as they become practically relevant to the management of her gender identity. Reciprocally, studies of physical examinations would include such special problems as Agnes's anxious modesty only as they are practically relevant to the organization of physical examinations.[1] What is the central theme, and the practically relevant context, is relative to the purpose of the study. As a collection, the various studies provide background for one another.[2] Finally, in elaborating how a theme is sustained in a social setting, verbal and nonverbal behavior are both discussed. The overall result is detailed description of how a wide variety of activities contribute to organizing one theme in a setting. The social context of the activities must also be described in some detail because it gives the indexical practices the particular sense they have in that setting.

In contrast, conversation analysts typically abstract a single communication practice, or small family of related practices, and explore the normative structure that that practice imposes on accounting and practical reasoning on any topic, in any setting. The practices are, almost exclusively, ways of talking. So long as the appropriate practices are employed in the conversations studied, there is no need for the conversations to have occurred in a single setting or among a single group of individuals. Any conversations will do. For example, if one wanted to analyze the practices by which strangers are introduced to one another by mutual friends or acquaintances, one could gather conversations occurring in any group and on any topic, as long as they included such introductions. Second, the substance of the conversation (even in the limited sense of requiring introductions to occur) are only sometimes relevant to analysis. For example, Sacks, Schegloff, and Jefferson (1978) analyze how turns at speaking are coordinated in conversation. Turn-taking occurs in all conversation. Conversation on any topic will do as data. Third, the situation in which the talk occurs is not necessarily relevant. Studies of turn-taking, for example, can sample conversations that occur in any situations that are convenient. Sometimes, though, the setting of the conversation is a factor in the selection of data

[1]   Emerson (1975) has done detailed studies of interaction between gynecologists and their patients from the perspective of its consequences for the organization of gynecological examinations. In her study, the origins of the patients' anxieties and fears are addressed only peripherally. Only the expression and control of anxiety in the examination itself, as a condition of sustaining the medical definition of the examination, are addressed systematically. Thus, in important respects, her study is a mirror image of Garfinkel's (1967) discussion of Agnes's experiences with doctors and provides context for it.

[2]   See J. Handel (1979) for a discussion of the methodological implications of this reciprocity among field studies.

and sets limits to the generality of the findings. For example, Schegloff (1979) has studied greetings in telephone conversations. In some respects, telephone conversations differ from face-to-face ones because supplementary nonverbal information is not available to the speakers. Thus, telephone greetings have some characteristic features, and care must be taken not to overgeneralize from them.

The overall effect of this approach is to limit studies to the verbal component of conversation without systematic discussion of the context in which the talk occurs. Very detailed attention is paid, instead, to the exact phrasing of messages, the placement of pauses and their effects, the fate of interruptions, signals in the talk that a new speaker will be chosen, regular sequences in the talk (such as question and answer), and so on. Transcripts of conversations are generally provided as illustrations of the analysis, and the normative rules ordering the conversation are specified in more detail and variety than is found in other ethnomethodological studies.

Conceptually, conversation analyses complement the studies of practical reasoning. In use, conversation is an indexical component of accounting practices. Talking is an accounting practice with its own rules. In effect, to engage in conversation is to perform a specific social role. This role can be performed simultaneously with virtually every other social role. Agnes talked. The police talked. The drug users talked. To understand fully how each role imposes contingencies on the other, each must be understood in its own right.

Conversation analysts study talk wherever it occurs, whatever it is about, whatever accompanies it. Studies of practical reasoning examine how socially defined themes are sustained in particular settings by a variety of practices, including talk. Ultimately, if both approaches to research continue, it should be possible to specify the social organization of settings and to differentiate the effects of the rules of conversation from those of other practical circumstances of the setting.

GENERAL RULES OF CONVERSATION

Conversational analysts argue that conversation, regardless of context and content, displays regularities of form. The term conversation is used, as Schegloff puts it (1968, pp. 1075-1076), to include "chats as well as service contacts, therapy sessions as well as asking for and getting the time of day, press conferences as well as exchanged whispers of 'sweet nothings.'" To account for the observed behavioral regularities, normative rules are posited that, if followed by conversationalists, would produce the regular behavior. These rules are intended as part of an adequate model of the actor. The specific interests and situation of the actors must be added to these rules describing how conversation should be ordered to account for the specific content of each conversation.

Taking Turns

Sacks, Schegloff, and Jefferson (1978) specify rules for taking turns in conversation that are asserted to be invariant, to apply in all conversation. The rules are formulated in a way that accounts for three gross behavioral regularities of conversation. First, almost always, only one person speaks at a time. Second, the turns at talking are orderly. Third, the transition from one turn to the next is orderly. These three regularities, they suggest, are the most fundamental regular features of conversation.

Their detailed examination of a large number of conversations showed that it is common for two speakers to talk simultaneously but that these overlaps are typically very brief.[3] Transitions from one speaker to another occur in the majority of cases, with only slight gaps or overlaps in talk, or none at all. That is, the end of one person's turn and the beginning of another's turn are well coordinated. The order and length of turns within a conversation vary and so do the number of parties to a conversation and the lengths of conversations as a whole. The length of conversations, their content, and the distribution of turns are not worked out in advance. Instead, they are worked out by participants in the course of the conversation and by practices contained in the conversation. Some talk is discontinuous, punctuated by pauses or gaps. A variety of behavioral techniques is employed during conversations to distribute turns within them. When errors or violations of smooth turn-taking procedures occur, a variety of behavioral techniques is used to repair the trouble and sustain orderly conversation.

Having identified a group of behavioral regularities in conversation, Sacks, Schegloff, and Jefferson (1978) specify the normative rules that could account for them. They argue that the techniques for allocating turns are divided into two groups. Either the current speaker can select the next speaker or the next speaker can select himself or herself.[4] A few simple rules can order these two modes of turn-taking. Turns at talk include places, such as the asking of a question, at which a transition from one speaker to another is relevant. At such places, if the current speaker has selected the next speaker (by directing a question to him or her, for example), that person has the right and the obligation to take the next turn. No one else shares that right and obligation. If the speaker has not selected the next speaker (by addressing the question to anyone who can answer it, for example), the next speaker selects himself or herself by starting first. If no next speaker selects himself or herself in such a situation, the current speaker may, but need not, continue until another opportunity for

[3]   Schegloff (1968) points out that in groups larger than two people, when more than one person talks simultaneously for an extended period, we perceive that two conversations are occurring in the group.

[4]   The possibility of a third party's selecting a speaker is ignored. At least among groups of children, transitions are sometimes made by one person securing a turn for another. "Come on. Let Harry talk."

transition occurs. When that next opportunity occurs, the same three rules apply. Assuming that people can recognize the places at which transitions from one speaker to another are relevant, these three rules, if followed, would produce the observed regularities of turn-taking. They are not necessarily the only rules that could account for the phenomenon, but, in the strong sense that we discussed earlier, they are adequate.

The application of these rules requires a catalog of behavioral techniques that could serve to select speakers and repair difficulties caused by overlaps or gaps. In addition, to understand the application of these rules in actual conversations, we would need to know why the various options are exercised in particular ways. The practical reasoning of the speakers would be relevant to that task. Some of the behavioral techniques might be generally recognized; others are surely specific to certain settings. That is, the collection of behaviors that might serve to direct the transition from one speaker to another is loosely defined or indexical, even though the rule for using them is quite specific. Once again, practical reasoning remains effective in the application of a formal system. The interdependence of the two types of ethnomethodological studies arises from simultaneous existence of adequate formal rules and loose collections of behaviors that meet their conditions.

Getting a Conversation Started

Once a conversation is under way, a small group of norms distributes the turns at talking and produces smooth-flowing conversations. These rules give considerable control of the conversation to the speaker. Within possible normative limits of turn length, the speaker controls when the transition to a new turn will occur and can select the next speaker if he or she chooses. This normatively guaranteed control is a considerable resource for the speaker.[5] However, the normative ordering of turns assumes that a speaker has already been selected and that the conversation is under way. Somehow, people must determine who will be the first speaker and assume initial control of the conversation.

Schegloff (1968) studied the opening of conversations over the telephone. In all but one of five hundred recorded calls, the conversation was opened according to the rule that the person called speaks first. The initial turn is typically confined to a greeting, such as "Hello," after which the caller returns the greeting and introduces the first topic of discussion.

---

[5]   See Scheff (1975) for a discussion of how control of the conversation can be utilized to guide the substance of others' talk and the outcome of discussions. Scheff shows that psychiatrists' normative rights to determine what is a suitable answer to questions and to return the floor to patients for better answers leads patients to define their problems in psychiatrically meaningful ways. Lawyers' ability to hold the floor until they have explained the legal implications of various statements leads their clients to tell their stories in legally advantageous ways.

In the one deviant case, the person called picked up the phone but did not speak. After a pause of about one second, the caller said "Hello." Despite the overwhelming majority of cases in which the person called spoke first, Schegloff did not regard the rule as adequate. It did not account for the observed evidence. Instead, he reformulated the rule to include the deviant case and, in so doing, probably extended the generality of his analysis of openings beyond telephone conversations.

To accommodate the deviant case, Schegloff acknowledged the ringing of the telephone as the initial turn in the conversation. He argued that a ringing telephone is one of many ways in which one person may summon another to speak. In person, making eye contact, speaking to the other person, or tapping him or her on the shoulder could be used. These summonses normatively require an answer, and, when the summons is acknowledged, both parties have expressed a commitment to interact further. Thus, in effect, the caller opens the conversation, and, when the called person says the initial words of greeting, he or she is responding to a summons. A relatively long pause between picking up the phone and speaking a greeting produces a problematic situation. The phone has been picked up and someone is presumed to be holding it, but the summons to converse has not been fully acknowledged. When the caller says "Hello," the caller is repeating the summons in a new form. Until the summons is acknowledged, the conversation will not proceed. Over the phone, the acknowledgment must be spoken.

Schegloff's analysis is interesting in two respects. First, it recognizes a nonverbal event as the opening turn in conversation. Although he is concerned with the talk, he cannot make it fully explicable without reference to other accounting media. It is quite likely that, as analyses of talk become more detailed, the nonverbal context will be incorporated in additional ways. Already, for instance, conversation analyses occasionally refer to tones of voice, although not in a systematic way. Second, his explication of the different functions that can be served by the term "hello" illustrates the looseness of the application of rules. To understand even the word "hello," one must know when it occurs in the conversation. The word can serve to summon another to interact or to acknowledge the summons and commit one to further interaction. At least in old Sherlock Holmes movies, "hello" is also used as a mild exclamation of discovery to signal that a clue has been noticed.

Ending Conversations

Conversational exchanges must eventually be ended. The smooth termination of talk requires that the relevance of rules for allocating turns must be terminated. The parties to the conversation must agree, in effect, that it is no one's normatively protected turn to speak. The problem is not simply to stop talking. This could be accomplished by hanging up phones without warning, by abruptly turning one's back and walking away from a speaker, or by nodding off to sleep. The problem is to end the conversation smoothly and cooperatively, with all parties knowing and agreeing that it has ended and all parties ceasing to make normative claims on the attention of the others.

Schegloff and Sacks (1974) studied how people use signals in a conversation to coordinate its end. The termination of a conversation requires a sequence in which the parties to the conversation acknowledge its end. The acknowledgment is signaled by the exchange of appropriate terminal remarks. The collection of appropriate remarks is loosely defined and probably varies from group to group. Some examples are "good-bye," "'bye," "see you later," "later," "what it is," and "good night." The normative obligations of the people in the conversation to one another are changed by the exchange of terminal remarks. These terminal exchanges signal the end of a role relationship (engaging in conversation) and the irrelevance of its norms.

The closing exchange, however, is not sufficient to coordinate withdrawal from conversation. Rather, events occurring earlier in the conversation provide places in which terminal exchanges are appropriate, just as places are provided where the right to speak may be transferred from one person to another. One way of coordinating the end of conversation is the use of "preclosing" remarks. At the end of a topic, common phrases, such as "so," "well," or "okay," spoken with appropriate intonation, can serve to signal that the conversation can appropriately be ended. Participants then choose whether to terminate the conversation or to introduce another topic. This type of preclosing makes ending the conversation an accountable option because the topic is exhausted and no other one is introduced. Alternately, these preclosing signals make changing the subject an accountable option.

Other preclosing signals make ending the conversation an accountable option for other reasons. A person can announce, as part of the conversation, that he or she must attend to other matters that have priority over continuing to talk. For example, "I've got to go. I'll be late for dinner" can serve as a signal to begin terminating the conversation. Alternatively, one person can begin to terminate the conversation because of priorities or interests attributed to the other. "I'll let you get back to your studying," or "This call must be getting expensive," or "You must be tired after your trip" are examples. Truncated announcements may indicate that a person has reasons to end the conversation without specifying them. "I've got to get going" is an example.

The substance of these signals can be as varied as the practical interests that take priority over the extension of a particular conversation. Their candor, completeness, and explicitness can vary as widely as the intimacy of relationships and the privacy of conversational settings. They serve the common function, however, of signaling the end of conversation accountably, and without giving offense to others.

Even earlier in conversation, remarks may be made that provide a temporal reference for the length of the conversation. Remarking on the lateness of a phone call or its closeness to dinner time may serve to justify the briefness of the call, independent of specific reasons to end it and of the exhaustion of topics to discuss. Such remarks provide a frame of reference for decisions concerning how long to speak on a topic, their order of introduction, how many topics to expect to cover, and whether to treat possible closing places as such. Knowing that a conversation will be brief, a person might decide to save complex topics for another time or be sure to raise important topics early.

The smooth termination of conversation, then, is dependent upon the exchange of signals throughout the conversation. The minimal requirement is that one party provide a practical reason to terminate the conversation at a particular time and that all parties acknowledge the end of conversation with appropriate closing remarks. Earlier parts of the talk may provide temporal references for the appropriate length of the conversation, with or without specific reasons. While the rest of the work of the conversation is being accomplished, this organizational matter is generally resolved without being noticed.

STRATEGIC OPPORTUNITIES PROVIDED BY NORMATIVE STRUCTURE

Thus far, we have discussed normative structures that regulate all conversations. Every conversation must begin and end. Between beginning and ending, people take turns speaking. Other normative regulations do not apply to every conversation. When they become applicable, however, they regulate conversation in at least two distinct ways. First, it may be optional whether to initiate a kind of talk which, once it has been initiated, imposes a normatively governed sequence on participants. For example, one need not, but may, ask a question. Once the question has been asked, however, it is normatively required that the subsequent sequence of talk culminate in an answer. Second, there may be quite general rules for how a topic is to be discussed, if it is discussed at all. Raising the topic is optional, but, by raising it, normative rules are imposed on the conversation.

These normative rules are strategic resources that people use as needed in conversation. When one wants information, one may, but need not, get it by asking a direct question. The question can be relied upon to evoke an answer. It may also reveal one's ignorance, express impolite interest in a topic, embarrass the person asked or asking, or reveal the asker's intentions. Speakers are free to ask or not to ask questions, to seek information or do without it, as their practical purposes dictate. The normative constraints imposed upon conversation by, for example, questions, and the consequent predictability of the response to them, make the initiation of sequences that are optional but regulated a reliable tool.

Identifying People

Conversations need not include reference to people who are not present, but they often do. When people are discussed, it is necessary to identify them. A variety of forms of identification apply to any person and can be used to establish who is being discussed. I am Warren or Dr. Handel. I am Ethan's father and Judy's husband. I teach out at SIUE. Some people identify me as a friend. I'm the guy who wrote this book. I am a former paper boy. Every mail-order business in the country seems to have identified me as a mail-order consumer. Any fact about me, or about any person, could be used to identify me (or him or her) in certain situations. It is not the importance of the fact that matters but its utility in establishing the person's identity in a particular conversation among particular people with particular prior knowledge. Sacks and Schegloff (1979) discuss the norms that regulate the identification of people in and for conversations.

The substance of the identifying form is not normatively regulated. The form of identification, however, is constrained by two normative preferences, which occasionally conflict. The conflict between the two preferences is resolved in a normatively constrained way. The first norm is a preference that identification be accomplished with a single reference form. The second norm is that, if possible, clear recognition of who is being discussed should be established.

Following the two norms simultaneously, a person will attempt to establish recognition with a single reference form rather than listing several identifying facts about the person being discussed. If the hearer signals that he or she recognizes who is being discussed, the sequence is complete. No more will be said to identify the person, although specific things about him or her may be discussed. If the hearer signals lack of recognition, another form of recognition is attempted. Again, rather than describing the person fully, a single fact will be introduced. In such cases, the norms that give preference to clear recognition and the use of single reference forms are in conflict. Second, and subsequent, forms are employed because the preference for clear recognition is the stronger of the two. Additional reference forms are employed one at a time because the preference for single forms is not dropped when the initial attempt fails. Instead, it is modified to a preference for establishing recognition with one more form. Ultimately, either clear recognition is achieved and signaled or the parties signal one another that establishing recognition is not worth continued effort. Either signal terminates the sequence, allowing the conversation to proceed.[6]

These norms provide strategic resources in at least two ways. First, if people are a topic of conversation, these norms allow their identity to be estab-

[6] Apparently, double reference forms such as "my dog, Spot," which includes the name and the relationship of possession, or "my son, the doctor," are normatively deviant and infrequent. Otherwise, it would be more parsimonious to formulate a single norm which gives a normative preference to establishing clear recognition with as few forms as possible. At each step in the sequence, speakers would decide which forms, and how many, would most efficiently identify the person.

138

lished in a quick, coordinated way. Second, the freedom of the speaker to choose the identifying form allows the selection to serve purposes other than those of simple identification. For example, the discretion to choose identifying forms is an important resource for keeping secrets in conversation and for communicating quite different messages simultaneously to different hearers, depending on their contextual knowledge of the person being discussed.

Consider talk about the person John Smith, a college student who lives on Elm Street, drives the old Edsel with the "Nuke the Discos" bumper sticker, used to date Emily, and pays his bills by selling illegal drugs on a small scale to friends. Any of these facts can identify him accurately. Let us send John on a trip to Florida and discuss it in a casual way with other acquaintances. This news will be interesting gossip, but it will have different implications for those who know he sells drugs than for those who do not know this fact. By not identifying John as a drug dealer, and not specifying the purpose of the trip, this news can be discussed in a group whose members are not all aware of his means of livelihood. To some, it will sound like a nice vacation; to others, a resupply mission.

The normatively preferred limitation of identification forms makes the omission of important identifying facts unnoticeable. Speakers can identify people without telling all that they know, and without revealing that they are holding anything back, so that speakers' trust of hearers does not become an issue. Hearers' knowledge about the person allows them to fill in their contextual knowledge and to receive information that is never mentioned. The hearer may even know more about the person than the speaker and may get more information from what is said than the speaker intends. The freedom to select the form of identification, coupled with the normative preference for brief identification, allows secrets to be preserved and allows hearers to assess the practical relevance of news in the contexts of their diverse knowledge.

The selection of identification forms can also communicate an attitude toward the person being discussed and establish which of the many facts about the person are relevant for the ongoing conversation. The form of identification may also signal something about the relationship between the people in the conversation. Identifying John Smith as a drug dealer, for example, reveals one's knowledge of such matters and can be used as a sign of trust and intimacy between speaker and hearer. The identifying form, then, provides a factual bit of information about the person being discussed. The choice of one form from among all the possibilities communicates other news as well.

Directing Remarks at Particular Others

By examining videotapes of a conversation among four people, Goodwin (1979) was able to establish two relatively simple norms that govern the addressing of remarks to particular others in groups by the coordination of gaze with talk. If the remark is directed at a particular person, the gaze of the speaker should be directed at that person while speaking. When talk is directed in this way, eye contact should be made while gazing at the other person. These two norms allow remarks to be addressed to a particular person in a discriminable way and provide eye contact as a signal to acknowledge that the direction of the remarks is recognized.

This normative arrangement can also be put to other purposes. Gazing at a person may be an end in itself or a means to initiate further interaction. The normative right to gaze and establish eye contact can be established by speaking to the subject on any topic. The gaze and eye contact, not the talk, may be important. Asking for the time, then, or for directions, justifies eye contact which can then be exploited to signal other intentions.[7]

Formulating the Conversation

During a conversation, people may sum up what the conversation has been about, its purpose, or its implications. These capsule summaries are, at once, about the conversation and part of it. They are called formulations. No simple set of norms that regulates formulations has been specified because formulations take a wide variety of forms. However, Heritage and Watson (1979) point out that formulations normatively require a sequence (in a form appropriate to the formulation) that acknowledges the formulation and signals whether it is accurate or not. In a conversation including reference to several events, for example, the time sequence may be formulated. "All this happened last weekend, right?" could serve as a formulation of when the events took place, over what time span, and so on. Since this formulation employs a question, the sequence will culminate in an answer. The answer either confirms or denies the accuracy of the formulation. The formulation might take the form of an exclamation. "Wow! That must have been a busy weekend!" could serve to formulate the timing of the events. "Yeah" would acknowledge the accuracy of the time reference and the business of the weekend. "It wasn't that busy" would confirm the timing, but not the level, of excitement.

Formulations serve many strategic ends. One is to help people keep track of the content of conversations and confirm that they share an understanding of it with others. A very important function of formulations is to make the content of the formulation normatively binding on participants. Once a formulation has been suggested and acknowledged, all parties to the conversation are normatively accountable to respect that version of the conversation. One especially important function of accountability to an explicit formulation of the content of a conversation is to coordinate actions subsequent to the conversation. In our discussions of practical reasoning, it became clear that categorizing events often implies a course of action, even if the course of action is not made explicit. Agreeing to the accuracy of a formulation binds people to courses of action

---

[7]   Goffman (1971) discusses many variations on this strategy.

appropriate to the formulation. Thus the formulation can provide reassurance that others will act in preferred ways or warnings that they may not. Sometimes, the formulation can bring normative pressure to bear on oneself by establishing a public and normative commitment to a line of action. People who reveal New Year's resolutions to others in hopes of establishing an extra incentive to keep them are using that strategy.

COMMUNICATING CONTENT THROUGH FORM

Content can be communicated in conversation by the manner of speaking, independently of the topics explicitly discussed. Some preliminary work has been done along these lines with respect to the display of sex roles in conversation. A number of studies have shown differences between the ways in which men and women respond to each other. The work is preliminary in two senses. First, the norms governing the observed regularities have not been specified yet. Second, the exact theme expressed in the behavioral differences is not clear. The theme is related to the conversational display of male dominance, but the evidence does not yet support a precise specification.

Fishman (1978) gathered her data by placing a tape recorder in the apartments of three couples. The couples controlled when the recorder operated and recorded themselves for continuous periods ranging from one to four hours. The resulting tape recordings were of ordinary conversations around the house. Although the sample of couples was small, prohibiting generalization, the rareness of such detailed data concerning everyday talk makes the study valuable.[8]

Fishman (1978) found that the women asked questions approximately three times as often as the men. Questions are among the conversational resources that oblige others to respond. That is, they tend to ensure that the conversation will continue, at least until an answer is given. Conversation can be opened with a type of question that normatively obtains the right to speak for the asker. "Know what?" and "Do you know what?" were common forms of this type of opening in her data. Normatively, the person who is asked such opening questions must respond with another question such as "No, what?" The original questioner is then normatively entitled to introduce a topic. The women used this attention-getting device twice as often as the men. Statements such as "This is interesting" also tended to initiate a question and answer sequence that culminated in the introduction of a topic. The women used this device more than the men. Openings such as "You know" are less reliable than the other attention-getting openings but still tend to start sequences leading to

---

[8] The detailed data make a very impressive case study of talk around a few homes. Sampling issues arise when we want to generalize the results of sex role behavior throughout our society. Other studies indicate that the conversations are typical.

the introduction of a topic. The women used this sort of opening eleven times as often as the men. Minimal, monosyllabic responses such as "yeah," "umm," and "huh" function in two different ways. At the end of someone's statement, they discourage further interaction. At short pauses during a turn at talk, they encourage the speaker to continue. The women's short responses tended to occur during men's turns at talk and to encourage the men to continue. The men's short responses tended to occur at the end of women's turns at talk and to discourage further talk. The men used direct statements twice as often as the women. The women almost always responded to the men's statements, but the men did not respond to the women as predictably.

In general, then, the women talked in ways that tended to extend conversation on any topic, both by encouraging men to continue and by introducing their own topics in ways that appended two or three turn sequences to their beginnings. Women's direct statements were not as successful in eliciting responses from men as men's statements were in eliciting responses from women. Fishman suggests that the indirect tactics are used by women because the direct tactics do not succeed as reliably for them. She also suggests that women do more of the "necessary work of interaction, starting conversations and then working to maintain them" (1978, p. 404). She concludes that women must do extra work to ensure that topics of their choice will be addressed in conversation because men, by their approach to conversation with women, express disinterest in what women have to say.

One interpretation of this asymmetrical distribution of the supportive work required to sustain conversation is that the men display dominance over the women by their manner of speaking. The conversational asymmetries are a reflection of the sex roles that operate in our society and are part of the operations by which those sex roles are sustained. Inequalities in conversational work are analogous to other inequalities, such as in rates of pay or employment opportunities. This interpretation gets some support from the observation that children utilize the same techniques in talking to adults that women use in talking to men (Fishman 1978). Children are known to have limited rights in conversation with adults, and those rights are defined by the adults by exercising the related rights to discipline children and teach them how to behave properly. If women are treated by men as children are treated by adults, and if women respond with conversational tactics similar to those used by children, it is reasonable to assume that they are being denied full adult rights in conversation.

West and Zimmerman (1977) investigated another conversational asymmetry that reflects directly on this interpretation of sex roles in conversation. They found that men interrupt women in two-party, cross-sex conversation more than women interrupt men. Interruptions are especially significant because they compromise the right of the speaker to complete turns at talk and determine the place where transitions to new speakers can occur. The interrupter simply takes the floor by speaking simultaneously with the speaker. This violates the fundamental norms that govern turn-taking and can be taken as direct proof that full rights are not being extended to the interrupted person. If men interrupt women more than women interrupt men, one can conclude that the women are not being granted equal rights to speak. The men are aggressively violating those rights, and/or by accepting the treatment, women are accepting or inviting their own subordination.

West and Zimmerman recorded conversations in a variety of settings. Some were between two men, some between two women, and some between a man and a woman. In the same-sex conversations, the interruptions were divided approximately equally between the two speakers. However, in the cross-sex conversations forty-eight interruptions occurred, of which forty-six were interruptions of women by men.[9] To confirm the observation that women's and children's speech tactics were similar, West and Zimmerman recorded parent-child interactions in a physician's office. Fourteen interruptions occurred. In twelve of the fourteen cases, the parent interrupted the child.

The women studied by West and Zimmerman did not react in an obviously negative way to being interrupted. In fact, after being interrupted, the women tended to be silent. West and Zimmerman tentatively concluded that the women's right to speak without interruption was routinely abridged by males without protest. West (1979) conducted another study to determine whether women accepted interruptions more passively than men did. In addition, she attempted to provide some support for the typicality of the earlier findings.

West recruited five male and five female subjects from an introductory sociology class. The subjects were previously unfamiliar with the other-sex person with whom they were paired in the experiment. They were told to relax and get to know one another prior to a more focused discussion of a campus problem chosen by the experimenter. The informal talks lasted twelve minutes. Since the subjects were strangers, politeness was expected to be relatively greater than among friends. That should have reduced the number of interruptions. In addition, although the sample was still small and not statistically random, the use of strangers suggested that regularities in the talk were the result of norms that were not peculiar to a small group of friends.

Twenty-eight interruptions occurred in the conversations. In twenty-one cases (75 percent) the male interrupted the female. West argues that, despite the different frequencies of interruption, the men and women responded similarly once interrupted. The most assertive response—continuing to talk simultaneously with the interruptor—was used after 14 percent of the interruptions by both males and females. Men interrupted by women finished their utter-

---

[9] To fully understand this asymmetry, it will be necessary to determine whether males interrupt each other more than females interrupt each other. Interruptions may be characteristic of male speech in all conversations, or they may occur more frequently when men talk to women than when they talk to other men. These are two quite different states of affairs.

ance briefly and then stopped in 43 percent of the cases. Women responded in that way about 38 percent of the time. Males interrupted by women stopped without finishing their utterances in 43 percent of the cases. Women showed this response after 48 percent of their interruptions by men. A larger sample is needed for a more thorough statistical appraisal, but the observed rates of response are not grossly different. This similarity suggests that the women do not accept interruption in a particularly passive way, and it undermines the argument that women accept, or even invite, dominance by men in conversation.

Other aspects of West's analysis are less clear in their implications. While the immediate response of the men and women were similar, the ultimate fate of the interrupted topics showed some asymmetry by sex. In a small percentage of cases (14 percent for men, 10 percent for women), the interrupted speaker reintroduced the interrupted topic later in the conversation. But, after interrupting a man, the women reintroduced his interrupted topic later in 43 percent of the cases. Men reintroduced women's interrupted topics in only 19 percent of the cases. As a result, only 43 percent of the males' topics were dropped after interruption, as compared with 71 percent of the females' topics. Women's and men's immediate responses to interruption were similar, but the results of the interruptions were quite different with respect to ending discussion of the interrupted topics. Thus, men's and women's responses to interruption, while behaviorally similar, are subject to different practical contingencies. Men can accept interruption gracefully, secure in the knowledge that the conversation will return to their chosen topic in the majority of cases; women must accept interruption gracefully despite the fact that 71 percent of their chosen topics will not be reintroduced. This result is quite similar to those reported by Fishman (1978).

These studies of asymmetries between men's and women's manners of speaking demonstrate clearly that conversational style is an important accounting medium. However, even if we grant that the observed asymmetries are typical, there are many unresolved empirical questions about them. For example, it is not clear whether women acquiesce in the abridgment of their rights relative to men's. The inconclusiveness of the research indicates the importance of carrying through the analyses of observed regularities until the norms underlying the observed behavior can be specified adequately. To illustrate the importance of that step of the analysis and the related step of specifying the practical reasoning by which the conduct and norms are related to one another, I should like to speculate about a possible set of norms that could account for all the conversational asymmetries just discussed.

It is important to remember that the asymmetrical conduct and its implication of male dominance are not necessarily intended or recognized. The regularities were only observed after careful examination of tape recordings, and their implications remain unclear even after considerable research. The norms that are followed in conversation may be quite unrelated to the theme of male dominance, even if they promote it. The connection among the norms, the manner of speaking, and their thematic implication may be concealed in the process of practical reasoning. Even people who are aware of the cultural theme of male dominance, even those who also approve of the arrangement, need not recognize that they act out and display that arrangement in conversation. Nor do they need to be aware of the asymmetrical conduct of men and women, even apart from its implications.

The speaker's control of turns at talk must apply only within loosely defined limits of how long talk has proceeded. After all, the right to hold the floor in conversation is not open ended. Once having begun speaking, a person cannot normatively command our attention forever by never providing a place where another speaker could begin or where the conversation could be ended. The length of turns, the number of turns that a person may take during a conversation, the number of topics that a person may introduce, and so on, must all be normatively limited in some way so that speakers will not impose too long on the attention of their audiences and so that audiences can extricate themselves accountably from conversations with people who talk too long or about too many things, and so on. We cannot quantify the norm at this time, but speakers and hearers must follow rules such as (1) continuing to speak or encouraging others to speak until enough has been said and (2) stopping the talk or encouraging others to stop speaking when enough has been said. These norms set upper and lower limits on the proper quantity of talk.

Suppose, now, that men and women define the word "enough" differently as it applies to various quantities of talk. If men, on average, preferred less talk[10] than women and if men and women applied the two conversation-limiting norms without attention to the sex of others in the conversation, all the observed phenomena would occur. Women would tend to talk more than men would prefer. That should lead to less frequent encouragement by men to continue, more interruptions by men, and less frequent follow-up by men on proposed topics. Men would tend to talk less than women would prefer. That should lead to fewer interruptions by women, to more frequent encouragement by women to continue, to more frequent follow-up by women on proposed topics, and to the reintroduction by women of their interrupted topics. Also, since these quantitative preferences are linked to gender, conversations between people of the same sex ought to display less asymmetry. People would still interrupt one another but would do so approximately equally.

Notice that the proposed norm does not call for different behavior toward the two sexes; nonetheless, it leads to that result. If the quantitative preferences are not recognized, the regularities, their factual connection to gender, and their implications could all go unnoticed. Each person, unaware of quantitative

---

[10] The quantity of talk might be measured directly or by some ratio such as time talking versus time listening or topics self-raised versus topics raised by others.

differences, could just be following the norms in accord with his or her own definition of "enough." If the gender-linked bias of the results are noticed at all, they could be experienced as a sense by men that women talk too much and a sense by women that men are secretive, cryptic, or too quiet. In addition to the quantities mentioned, preferences for the amount of talk in a given time period, for the frequency with which topics are reconsidered, and for the number of topics discussed in a given time period might also operate. Similar self-concealing reasoning processes could be generated by, for example, gender-linked preferences for different accounting media. Women might prefer talk, for instance, when men prefer nonverbal cues for the particular message and situation.

This speculative exercise is intended to make several points. First, it is imperative to complete these analyses. We must know what the observed regularities are, and we must also know how these regularities occur. Second, the operative norms may be quite different from their consequences. This is an important implication of the principle that practical reasoning is self-concealing. Given simple, unnoticed conditions, such as gender-linked preferences on any of a variety of quantitative dimensions, norms that apply equally to men and women may lead to differences between men's and women's behavior and their response to one another. Third, the principle that practical reasoning is self-concealing allows the analyst some discretion in specifying norms. Fourth, the principle also suggests an obligation to specify how the norms could operate without notice, unless there is evidence that they are known to actors.

AN EXPERIMENTAL PROCEDURE FOR SPECIFYING THE IMPORTANCE OF CONVERSATIONAL RESOURCES

This discussion of conversational norms has distinguished between norms that are invariantly applicable and norms that are only occasionally relevant. Various optional conversational techniques may all be useful, but not all are necessary to conversation or equally valuable. Kent, Davis, and Shapiro (1978) devised an experimental technique to assess the function of questions in structuring and restructuring conversations. Some evidence indicates that their procedure can be adapted to the investigation of other conversational techniques. If that proves true, it should be possible to differentiate the functions of different conversational techniques and to assess their relative importance for organizing conversations.

Kent, Davis, and Shapiro divided experimental subjects into three groups. In one group, pairs of subjects held unconstrained conversations. In the second, the subjects were instructed not to ask questions or to imply them by the intonation of their talk. The loss of questions as a resource was expected to disrupt the conversation. To be sure that the disruption was due specifically to the absence of questions, and not just to the difficulty of unnatural style, a second control group was used. In that group, the use of subordinate clauses was forbidden, limiting the speakers to simple sentences. This was expected to be unnatural, but not to pose any difficulties in getting messages across. Although the subjects did not perfectly follow their instructions, the reduction of questions and subordinate clauses was statistically significant.

Questions have the effect, among other things, of turning over the floor to a new speaker for the purpose of providing an answer. Thus, a specific hypothesis of the study was that turns at talk would be longer when questions were not permitted. This hypothesis was borne out. The absence of subordinate clauses did not have this effect. On the other hand, the absence of subordinate clauses and of questions both tended to slow down the speed of talk relative to the unconstrained condition. The general effects of the difficulty of talking in an unnatural manner, then, could be differentiated from the effects of losing a particular resource.

More pervasive effects of the absence of questions were also demonstrated. The talk was transcribed, and each turn was typed on a separate card. The decks of cards were then shuffled and sorters were asked to reconstruct the conversation. Even after the ability to connect questions with their answers was controlled, the ability of sorters to reconstruct the questionless conversations was impaired. That is, without the use of questions, the conversation could not be returned to its original order. The talk was less organized.

The importance of this study lies in the contrast between the prohibitions of questions and of subordinate clauses. Both were difficult and caused the conversation to slow down. But only the prohibition of questions disrupted the structure of the conversation or altered the length of turns. We can conclude, then, that the prohibition of questions disrupts conversation more than the prohibition of subordinate clauses. In that sense, questions are the more important conversational resource. This design may allow the comparison of various conversational resources with respect to how difficult it is to conduct conversation without them, the specific nature of the problems generated by their absence, and their importance to orderly conversation.

This experiment also suggests that conversation analysis may have direct practical implications. If instructions can be designed that disrupt conversation in predictable ways, it is likely that instructions can be designed to improve conversational effectiveness as well. As the norms of conversation are identified, perhaps they can serve as the basis for training programs to develop special skills to systematically improve the routine conversational skills learned in more traditional and more haphazard ways.

SUMMARY

The detailed analysis of talk allows specific norms to be identified which can account for observed regularities. The application of these norms involves choice and requires the use of loosely defined categories. Thus, the normative regulation of talk is integrated with other aspects of practical reasoning and accounting. Both the exercise of choice and the looseness of categories provide strategic opportunities for people in conversations. Some relate directly to the substance and organization of the talk itself. Others relate to other practical concerns. In addition, the norms and the consequences of following them can be self-concealing and have important unnoticed effects. This makes the completion of analyses of social regularities by specifying the operative norms and the reasoning through which they are applied imperative. This is another demonstration of the importance of practical reasoning and detailed analysis of accounts for understanding and explaining social regularities.

SUGGESTED READINGS

Additional conversational analyses are conveniently collected by Psathas (1979), Schenkein (1978), and Sudnow (1972).

7

The Standpoint of This Study

It is characteristic of sociology that each group of specialists in the discipline emphasizes its differences from the others and from sociology as a whole. In technical writing, sociologists recognize and account for this phenomenon by referring to sociology as a multiparadigm discipline.[1] The phenomenon is readily observable by beginning students, too. If you have read an introductory textbook, you have probably noticed that the author respected and contributed to the subdivision of sociology by topic, by the size of the system studied, by the methodological techniques employed, and by theoretical commitments. Introductory textbooks do not describe the social world in authoritative, sociological terms. Rather, they describe what several competing sociological specialties have to say about it. If you have had several sociology courses, you probably also have had difficulty establishing intellectual continuity as you changed topics and instructors. Don't blame yourselves. Sociology really is a higgledy-piggledy assembly of specialties, and the overall pattern of the discipline really is crazy quilt. We love the things we love for what they are.

In my opinion, and you should know that it is not a very widely shared opinion, the differences among sociological specialties are greatly exaggerated and consist primarily of miscommunication caused by jargon. This book was written from the standpoint that ethnomethodology is a sociological specialty that can be logically integrated with the rest of the discipline and ought to be for good practical reasons. This opinion has intentionally influenced my presentation in two ways. (1) This is a short book (although sometimes writing it seemed endless to me), and it was necessary to be selective in coverage. As much as I could without misrepresenting ethnomethodology, my selections were intended to facilitate the integration of knowledge about ethnomethodology with other sociological knowledge. (2) Whenever I encountered ambiguity in the literature, I interpreted sociology and ethnomethodology as compatible with one another.

One of the privileges of academic authorship is the opportunity to pontificate about the direction that future research should take. Of all the intellectual challenges facing ethnomethodology and sociology in general, I believe that the integration of existing knowledge in a coherent and useful form is the most pressing. Until that is done, sociologists will be unable to communicate with one another; the recruitment and training of students will be impaired; and the utility of sociology for a society that increasingly relies upon intelligent central planning will be diminished. In the remaining few pages, I shall indicate how

[1] See, for examples Wilson (1970) and Wagner (1974). As one would expect in a multiparadigm science, the nature of the paradigmatic divisions is not agreed upon. "Paradigm" is used as a technical term by sociologists, loosely following its definition by Thomas Kuhn (1962) in his discussion of the history of science. A paradigm can be understood as a normative model, sustained in a scientific community, of how science should be done.

jargon operates as a self-concealing protection against precise sociological communication and how ethnomethodology might be integrated with the rest of sociology.

JARGON

Every scientific discipline and specialty develops its own terminology. At best, these specialized languages allow efficient, abbreviated communication within the verbal community. Ordinarily, a lengthy period of training is required to understand and use these terms. During this training, one also becomes accredited and earns the normative right to participate in the community of scientists. These specialized languages exclude the untrained. Without training, one can neither understand technical jargon nor use it to communicate with scientists or technicians. Without training, one has no right to be heard on scientific subjects or to evaluate the practice of science. At least one has no such rights within the scientific community. Jargon can excommunicate as well as communicate.

Sociological jargon, however, has developed in such a way that, by communicating in technical terms, each narrow group of specialists excludes the rest of the discipline and the scientific community. No concise, precise communication is supported, with the possible exception of the jargon describing mathematical research procedures. Sociological terminology has two peculiar characteristics that contribute to this situation. First, each specialty tends to develop new terms for its concepts, even when appropriate terms already exist elsewhere in the discipline.[2] Second, each specialty tends to define shared terms in different ways.[3]

The self-concealment of assumptions through jargon operates in a relatively straightforward way. Various groups of specialists use the same term, for example "power," to refer to different phenomena. Each group makes statements about power that are accurate, perhaps, for the phenomenon it calls power but inaccurate for the phenomena that other groups call power. Since each group "knows what power is" and assumes that the other groups also know, the definitional differences are not carefully considered. Each group tends to think

[2] For comparison, consider the technical terms used for the chemical elements. Different specialists may be familiar with different aspects of chemistry, but all use the same names for the same chemicals. Imagine what communication problems would arise if different specialists used the term oxygen for different elements and, at the same time, used different terms for the same elements. For some, then, the abbreviation H_2O would mean water; for others, F_eO might be the abbreviation for salt, whereas water would be F_2Cl.

[3] Gibbs (1965; 1966) has reviewed and organized various uses of the terms "norm" and "sanction" by sociologists. Nagel (1968) discusses several variations in the use of the term "power." These three are among the most fundamental and commonly used terms in sociology. The degree to which sociologists differ on the proper definition of these terms is indicative of the state of our terminology.

that the others are making incorrect statements about the same phenomenon rather than statements about different phenomena. When the definitional differences are noticed, reconciliation tends to take the form of (1) assuming that the various uses of the term are closely related and refer to different aspects of the same phenomenon and (2) generating additional definitions that are sufficiently vague to include the others. Since these additional terms are not adopted throughout the discipline, each attempt to simplify terminology has the effect of further complicating it. The use of numerous unshared technical terms conceals the information that might let researchers notice that they are discussing different phenomena but are using the same term. And, of course, the use of varied unshared terms conceals the fact that researchers are often discussing the same phenomena but are using different terms.

COMPATIBILITY OF ETHNOMETHODOLOGY AND SOCIOLOGY

Implications of the Rule of Adequacy

Ethnomethodologists accept adequacy, in the sense discussed in Chapter 2, as a goal and as a criterion for evaluating theory. The commitment to an adequate theory, or to constructing an adequate model of the actor, implies that there can be no contradiction between ethnomethodological theory and any accountably accurate empirical sociological finding. Among other requirements, an adequate model of the actor must be programmed to reproduce all observed regularities of social behavior. The actor must be programmed to pass unnoticed among people.

As we have seen, regularities of behavior are specific to the procedures by which they are observed. Different procedures (or practices, or standpoints, or methods) result in different accounts of events, each account suitable to only some situations. One way to observe human behavior is to participate in group life and view events in the commonsense manner of the group and the situation. The adequate model of the actor must be programmed to behave in a way that is accountably normal when observed in that way. Another way to observe human behavior is to select a sample of respondents, administer a questionnaire to the sample, and statistically assess regularities in the responses. The adequate model of the actor must be programmed to reproduce the regularities observed in this way, too. A sample of programmed actors, or a computer simulation of such a sample, should answer questionnaires indistinguishably from a sample of people. A sample of actors, or a simulation of such a sample, should also be indistinguishable from a sample of experimental subjects (or a laboratory small group, or a subculture) when both are examined in the same way. Every empirical finding that is accountable in the sociological community then must be compatible with an adequate model of the actor.

This does not mean that ethnomethodology must attend to the results of questionnaires (or other sociological findings) in the same way as other sociologists do or that ethnomethodology must become social psychological. Far from it. Ethnomethodology is most interesting and informative when it addresses assumptions that are, in addition to being unnoticed, protected from scrutiny by various social arrangements. Ethnomethodology is not committed to the view of attitude researchers, for instance, that when people make a checkmark on a piece of paper, some cognitive structure, or enduring tendency to act, or some disposition is revealed. However, in their own way, ethnomethodologists must account for why each person checks the paper where he or she does and why the population reveals the statistical regularities among checkmarks that it does.

Problems Posed by the Necessity to Make Assumptions

Carroll's report of the conversation between the tortoise and Achilles proved that assumptions must be made between each step of a formal argument. Put another way, arguments don't consist of steps. They consist of leaps of faith. Carroll does not specify the exact nature of the assumptions required. Probably they can be formulated in many ways. However they are formulated, their effect is recognition that an argument is obviously clear and complete as it stands and exempt from further explication or examination. In making statistical arguments, or arguments in a traditional, logical format, sociologists must make those assumptions. Ethnomethodologists, however, want to treat those assumptions as the topic of inquiry. Will this necessarily create some incompatibility between the two approaches to social life? Can ethnomethodology eliminate the assumptions?

I think not. Ethnomethodologists explicate the practical concerns and substantive assumptions that underlie routine activities. From these materials, they have begun to specify the formal structure of practical reasoning. But, if Carroll's proof is to be taken seriously (and every proof should be taken seriously until some accountable reason is found to declare that it is not complete and clear as it stands), then, no matter how detailed the explication of practical reasoning becomes, there will be assumptions left implicit at every step in the reasoning. In addition, the ethnomethodologist's own account of practical reasoning must also continue to rest on unstated assumptions. The crux of the matter, then, is the substance of the assumptions. Are the assumptions that establish and normatively enforce the adequacy of arguments in traditional logic different from the ones that underlie practical reasoning? There is no reason to think so. Ethnomethodologists have found the same formal properties when they studied social scientific presentations, practical reasoning, and their own arguments. Provisionally, we can assume, then, that, when people recognize argument of any form as adequate, the fundamental assumptions required for that recognition are always the same.

Ethnomethodology will be no more assumption free than any other enterprise. It cannot be. In every step of every argument, ethnomethodologists will rely on assumptions too. So far as we can tell, even while describing those assumptions, ethnomethodologists continue to make them. There is an important implication in this for the selection of data. Except for convenience, there does not seem to be anything to recommend any source of data as especially suited to examining practical reasoning and the assumptions underlying it. Specifically, one does not get closer to those assumptions by studying the process of uncovering them. They continue to be required in each argument and appear again in the same form. Like everyone else, then, ethnomethodologists must make assumptions to argue convincingly. Any data will do, so they might as well be interesting and important. Having clearly demonstrated that the reflexivity of accounts extends to ethnomethodological studies, ethnomethodologists can study their own activities less and the activities of more important groups more without compromising standards of research. No one can do more than to argue clearly enough for now and get on with it. Anyone who tries to surpass that standard is doomed to fail. This does not imply that efforts to argue more clearly or to further specify our assumptions should be slackened. It does imply, however, that arguments can not be discounted because they rest on unspecified assumptions. All arguments do. An argument is good enough for now until assumptions are explicated and shown to require a reduction in our confidence in the argument.

Problems Posed by the Distinctive Formal Structure of Practical Reasoning

Ethnomethodologists intend, ultimately, to formulate a theory that is radically different from other sociological theories. The intended crux of the difference is the incorporation of the distinctive formal structure of practical reasoning in sociological theory. The differences between practical reasoning and traditional logic have been acknowledged by scholars for more than two thousand years. The Latin terms used to describe them have been in continuous use since Latin was a spoken language, and some of the characteristics of loose concepts had been recognized by the Greeks even before the rise of Rome. Ethnomethodologists, though, hope to address these characteristics in a distinctive way.

The social sciences require a model of how people think and perceive. This model allows predictions to be made concerning how humans will respond to events. Even thorough behaviorists, who reject the terminology of perception and thought as mental, acknowledge information processing. Most of the models of how humans think and perceive use traditional logic or mathematical equations as foundations. Traditional logic serves as a standard for rational thought and conduct. It is recognized that people are not always rational, however, and the models account for deviations from rational behavior as errors. The effect is for theory to develop by appending more and more detailed corrections to the basic model of rationality. Ethnomethodologists want to replace traditional logic and the body of corrections with a formal structure that includes all the conduct and thinking in a straightforward way.

Clearly, if this intention is realized, the result would be a radical revision of social scientific theory. The statistical findings and theories concerning large-scale phenomena might be unaffected, but, wherever the theories touch upon human reasoning or explain large-scale events in terms of the results of decision-making, it would be transformed. In place of traditional logic and a set of corrections to explain how people deviate from strictly rational behavior, a new formal model would appear.

But that transformation of theory has not occurred yet. There is no guarantee that it will occur in the immediate future or even that improved formal models will come as a result of intentional efforts. Improved models might result, for example, in a serendipitous reformulation of all the corrections by researchers studying practical reasoning as flawed traditional logic. I am suggesting, then, that we distinguish among the possible future discrepancies between ethnomethodology and other sociological theories and those that exist now. I should like to suggest that, to date, the results of ethnomethodological research have not been incompatible with other sociological theories.

When ethnomethodologists study practical reasoning, it is a crucial part of their procedure to suspend judgment of the correctness of the reasoning. If people are observed to reason in a certain way, and their accounts and actions are acceptable to other participants in the situation, ethnomethodologists accept the accounts, reasoning, and action as acceptable in the situation. This procedure is vital to ethnomethodological research. It allows the researcher to identify accountable practical reasoning without first formulating rules of practical reasoning to serve as a model. The judgment, operationally considered, is not really suspended but, rather, is delegated to the subjects being studied. The researcher, by delegating judgment in this way, is able to collect instances of accountable practical reasoning before he or she is able to specify the standards by which they are judged accountable.

Once collected, these instances of accountable reasoning and action are used quite differently in ethnomethodological studies than they are in practical circumstances. Instead of using practical reasoning to explain and justify action, ethnomethodological studies take practical reasoning as their topic and attempt to specify its standards. To consider how this is done in detail, it will help to reconsider a specific study. Zimmerman (1970) found that receptionists in a public assistance agency assigned clients to intake workers by preparing a chart and entering the next client's name on the chart, following the rule "Fill the chart from top to bottom and then from left to right." A variety of circumstances led to violation of that normatively prescribed procedure, however. The receptionists did not anticipate these. But, when they occurred, the receptionists acted as if they were implied by the rule all along. In some instances they did not merely tolerate exceptions but, rather, actually expected exceptions to be made while still adhering to the rule as a general policy. Operationally, the procedure of suspending judgment allows one to recognize that these apparent exceptions are grounded in sound practical reasoning. However, delegating judgment makes observations like the following two improper. (1) The receptionist treated an event as an exception and no one reacted negatively to that treatment, but the event was not really an exception. (2) The receptionist followed the usual procedure, and no one objected to that action, but the case was exceptional and should have been treated as such.

By what standard are instances exceptional? The people being studied treated them as implied by the original rule and enforced exceptional behavior with sanctions when it was deemed appropriate. The standards by which exceptions are identified seem to be those of traditional logic. The researcher formulates a rule. He or she then observes conduct that could not be considered following the rule, if the rule is understood literally and logically. The researcher then specifies the practical circumstances that justify the exceptions to the rule and, assuming that the reasoning involved is correct, attempts to specify the formal properties of that reasoning. Operationally, then, the formal properties discovered by this procedure involve a contrast between traditional logic and actual reasoning. The contrast is not invidious. Rather, it establishes the conditions that an adequate model of practical reasoning must meet. Still, it is a contrast.

So long as these procedures are followed, the specification of formal properties in ethnomethodology will be compatible with other approaches that are based on contrasts with traditional logic. When ethnomethodologists are able to specify the formal structure of practical reasoning and specify what makes reasoning sound, they will be able to abandon this way of gathering data. Until that occurs, however, traditional logic is used as a resource in identifying exceptional practical reasoning. So long as traditional logic is used as a standard of rationality in this way, ethnomethodological theory will be compatible with that in the rest of sociology.

THE PRACTICAL UTILITY OF ETHNOMETHODOLOGY

Conversation analysis is the most clearly useful variant of ethnomethodology at the present state of development. As the normative rules governing conversation are specified in more detail, it should prove possible to base training programs on them. Nonnative speakers of a language, for example, Spanish-speaking Americans trying to use English, could be taught how to reduce their violation of conversational norms just as they are taught to reduce violation of grammatical ones. In turn, this should reduce the disruption they cause in conversation. For example, the signals that they are normatively obligated to acknowledge in American-English conversation could be presented. Polite patterns of eye contact could be learned. These same matters would be interesting to anyone who had specific conversational objectives and wanted to control conversations more effectively. For example, sales personnel could learn how to extend the length of conversations by structuring them so that refusals become impolite.

Studies of practical reasoning can also be put to practical use. Bittner (1967b) studied the conditions under which the police would categorize a person as mentally ill, apprehend the person, and take him or her to a hospital for psychiatric examination and possible commitment. He found that categorizing a person as mentally ill was a last resort, to be used only in extreme circumstances. The category was avoided because its use had negative practical implications for the officers. The bureaucratic rewards of police work are reserved for success in making arrests. Even if one becomes skilled in the resolution of family disputes and recognition of insanity, there is no career benefit to be derived. In addition, police are judged by their ability to bring cases to closure quickly. Apprehending the mentally ill is time-consuming because it involves the police in hospital procedures. In addition, the police lose control of their cases to doctors who may decide that the person is not mentally ill and must be returned to his or her home. For these reasons, formally categorizing a person as mentally ill and apprehending the person are resisted.

Suppose that policy concerning the apprehension of the mentally ill was being examined. Suppose, too, that officials were dissatisfied with police performance in this area. Officers in the field might be using the category too sparingly. A few acts of violence by people whom the police had declined to categorize as mentally ill could lead to that conclusion. Or the category might be employed too frequently. A few lawsuits by people taken to hospitals unwillingly and found sane could lead to that conclusion. Bittner's study is very suggestive as to how police conduct must be changed. Simply changing the formal definitions and policies will probably be ineffective. The reasons for applying or not applying the category are linked to the practical interests of the police. So, if we want them to reevaluate the situation, we must give them a practical reason to do so. In this case, the officers would have to be convinced that evaluations of their merits as police officers would reflect their use of this category. The category should be used more frequently, for instance, if officers were convinced that their careers would be enhanced by its use. This might require a change in the reward system in the police bureaucracy or an educational program for officers, or both. Bittner's analysis of the practical reasoning underlying the judgment of mental health suggests what we must do to change those judgments. Knowledge of practical reasoning in other settings can be put to analogous use.

This application of ethnomethodological studies does not depend on their specification of formal structures. However, it is likely that, as the formal properties of practical reasoning become more completely specified, the specifications will have practical utility as well. Suppose that we are convinced that bureaucratic rewards are the key to changing patterns of police decision making and that manipulating promotions and salary increases will be effective in getting officers to do what they think their superiors want. We would then face the problem of how to communicate our desires to the officers. Simply saying what we want them to do may not be effective. Their different situation may lead them to interpret our remarks in undesirable ways. In extreme cases, labor-management distrust may lead officers to look for hidden and harmful motives in every policy. If we knew, in detail, the formal characteristics of sound practical reasoning, we ought to be able to design a message that would be understood in the desired way. The ability to construct convincing practical arguments and thereby control what conclusions people will reach through practical reasoning could not help but be useful.

The utility of intellectual pursuits is not an incidental matter. In the opinion of many, it is the essence of their justification. Kant (1974, p. 3) states that "the aim of every step in the cultural process which is man's education is to assign this knowledge and skill he has acquired to the world's use." Robert Frost (1969, pp. 293-294) puts the matter succinctly and clearly. The last word in this volume belongs to him.

It's knowing what to do with things that counts.

Bibliography

Aronson, Elliot, and J. Merrill Carlsmith. 1968. "Experimentation in Social Psychology," in *The Handbook of Social Psychology*, Vol. 2 (2nd ed.), pp. 1-79, eds. Gardner Lindzey and Elliott Aronson. Reading, Mass., Addison Wesley.

Bar-Hillel, Yehoshua. 1954. "Indexical Expressions," *Mind* 63:359-379.

Bittner, Egon. 1967a. "The Police on Skid Row: A Study of Peace Keeping," *American Sociological Review* 32:699-715.

———. 1967b. "Police Discretion in Emergency Apprehension of Mentally Ill Persons," *Social Problems* 14:278-292.

Black, Max. 1970a. "Reasoning with Loose Concepts," *Margins of Precision*, pp. 1-13. Ithaca, N.Y.: Cornell University Press.

Black, Max. 1970b. "The Justification of Logical Axioms," *Margins of Precision,*" pp. 14-22. Ithaca, N.Y.: Cornell University Press.

Carroll, Lewis. "What the Tortoise Said to Achilles," in *The Complete Works of Lewis Carroll*, pp. 1225-1230. New York: Modern Library.

Churchill, Lindsey. 1971. "Ethnomethodology and Measurement," *Social Forces* 50:182-191.

Cicourel, Aaron. 1964. *Method and Measurement in Sociology.* New York: Free Press.

———. 1968. *The Social Organization of Juvenile Justice.* New York: Wiley.

———. 1974a. *Theory and Method in a Study of Argentine Fertility.* New York: Wiley.

———. 1974b. "Introduction," in *Language Use and School Performance*, pp. 1-16, ed. Aaron Cicourel et al. New York: Academic Press.

———, and John Kitsuse. 1963. *The Educational Decision Makers.* Indianapolis: Bobbs-Merrill.

Cicourel, Aaron, and John Kitsuse. 1963. *The Educational Decision Makers.* Indianapolis: Bobbs-Merrill.

Coser, Lewis. 1975. "Presidential Address: Two Methods in Search of a Substance," *American Sociological Review* 40:691-700.

Daly, Lloyd, ed. 1961. *Aesop Without Morals.* New York: Thomas Yoseloff.

Denzin, Norman. 1970. "Symbolic Interaction and Ethnomethodology," in *Understanding Everyday Life*, pp. 261-287, ed. Jack Douglas. Chicago: Aldine.

Douglas, Jack, ed. 1970. *Understanding Everyday Life.* Chicago: Aldine.

Edwards, Paul, ed. 1967. *The Encyclopedia of Philosophy.* New York: Macmillan.

Emerson, Joan. 1975. "Behavior in Private Places," in *Life as Theater*, pp. 329-343, eds. Dennis Brissett and Charles Edgley. Chicago: Aldine.

Emerson, Robert, and Melvin Pollner. 1976. "Dirty Work Designations: Their Features and Consequences in a Psychiatric Setting," *Social Problems* 23:243-254.

Fishman, Pamela. 1978. "Interaction: The Work Women Do," *Social Problems* 25:397-406.

Frost, Robert. 1969. "At Woodward's Gardens," in *The Poetry of Robert Frost*, pp. 293-294, ed., Edward Connery Lathem. New York: Holt, Rinehart and Winston.

Garfinkel, Harold. 1963. "A Conception of, and Experiments with, 'Trust' as a Condition of Stable Concerted Actions," in *Motivation and Social Interaction*, pp. 187-238, ed. O. J. Harvey. New York: Ronald Press.

———. 1964. "Studies of the Routine Grounds of Everyday Activities," *Social Problems* 11:225-250.

———. 1967. *Studies in Ethnomethodology.* Englewood Cliffs, N.J.: Prentice-Hall.

———, and Harvey Sacks. 1970. "On Formal Structures of Practical Actions," in *Theoretical Sociology*, pp. 337-366, eds. John McKinney and Edward Tiryakian. New York: Appleton-Century-Crofts.

Gibbs, Jack. 1965. "Norms: The Problem of Definition and Classification," *American Journal of Sociology* 70:586-594.

———. 1966. "Sanctions," *Social Problems* 14:147-159.

Goffman, Erving. 1959. *The Presentation of Self in Everyday Life.* Garden City, N.Y.: Anchor Books.

———. 1971. *Relations in Public.* New York: Basic Books.

Goodwin, Charles. 1979. "The Interactive Construction of a Sentence in Natural Conversation," *Everyday Language*, pp. 97-122, ed. George Psathas. New York: Wiley.

Gouldner, Alvin. 1954. *Wildcat Strike.* New York: Harper & Row.

Griffin, Donald R. 1976. *The Question of Animal Awareness.* New York: Rockefeller University Press.

Haire, Mason. 1968. "Projective Techniques in Marketing Research," in *Social Perception*, pp. 37-43, eds. Hans Toch and Henry Clay Smith. Princeton, N.J.: Van Nostrand.

Handel, Judith. 1979. "Using Participant Observation Research to Study Structural Phenomena," *Humanity and Society* 3:275-285.

Handel, Warren. 1979. "Normative Expectations and the Emergence of Meaning as Solutions to Problems: Convergence of Structural and Interactionist Views," *American Journal of Sociology* 84:855-881.

Hastorf, Albert, and Hadley Cantril. 1968. "They Saw a Game," in *Social Perception*, pp. 63-72, eds. Hans Toch and Henry Clay Smith. Princeton, N.J.: Van Nostrand.

Heritage, J. C., and D. R. Watson. 1979. "Formulations as Conversational Objects," in *Everyday Language*, pp. 123-162, ed. George Psathas. New York: Wiley.

Kant, Immanuel. 1974. *Anthropology from a Pragmatic Point of View*, trans. with an Introduction and Notes by Mary J. Gregor. The Hague: Martinus Nijhoff.

Kent, Gerald, John Davis, and David Shapiro. 1978. "Resources Required in the Construction and Reconstruction of Conversation," *Journal of Personality and Social Psychology* 36:13-22.

Kuhn, Thomas. 1957. *The Copernican Revolution.* New York: Vintage Books.

———. 1962. *The Structure of Scientific Revolutions.* Chicago: University of Chicago Press.

Leiter, Kenneth. 1974. "Ad Hocing in the Schools: A Study of Placement Practices in the Kindergartens of Two Schools," in *Language Use and School Performance,* pp. 17-75, eds. A. Cicourel et al. New York: Academic Press.

———. 1976. "Teachers' Use of Background Knowledge to Interpret Test Scores," *Sociology of Education* 49:59-65.

Lennon, John. 1973. "Review of Aaron Cicourel, *The Social Organization of Juvenile Justice,*" *Sociological Quarterly* 10:546.

Luckmann, Thomas. 1972. "Review of *Understanding Everyday Life,* edited by Jack Douglas," *Contemporary Sociology* 1:30-32.

Mannheim, Karl. 1964. "On the Interpretation of Weltanschauung," in *Essays on the Sociology of Knowledge,* pp. 33-83, ed. Karl Mannheim. Translated and edited by Paul Kecskemeti. London: Routledge and Kegan Paul.

Mawson, C. O. Sylvester. 1975. *Dictionary of Foreign Terms.* Revised and updated by Charles Berlitz. New York: Harper & Row, Pub.

Mayrl, William. 1973. "Ethnomethodology: Sociology Without Society," *Catalyst* 7:15-28.

McHugh, Peter. 1968. *Defining the Situation.* Indianapolis: Bobbs-Merrill.

McLeod, Ross. 1975. "Doing Snogging," *Urban Life and Culture* 3:442-445.

Mead, G. H. 1964. "A Pragmatic Theory of Truth," in *Selected Writings,* pp. 320-345, ed. George Herbert Mead. Introduction by Andrew Reck. Indianapolis: Bobbs-Merrill.

Melbin, Murray. 1969. "Behavior Rhythms in Mental Hospitals," *American Journal of Sociology* 74:650-665.

Merton, Robert. 1957. "The Role-Set: Problems in Sociological Theory," *British Journal of Sociology* 8:106-120.

———. 1968. *Social Theory and Social Structure,* enlarged ed. New York: Free Press.

Miller, Arthur G., ed. 1972. *The Social Psychology of Psychological Research.* New York: Free Press.

Moerman, Michael. 1966. "Kinship and Commerce in a Thai-Lue Village," *Ethology* 5:360-364.

Nagel, Jack. 1968. "Some Questions About the Concept of Power," *Behavioral Science* 13:129-137.

Orne, Martin, and Karl Scheibe. 1964. "The Contribution of Nondeprivation Factors to the Production of Sensory Deprivation Effects: The Psychology of the 'Panic Button,' "*Journal of Abnormal and Social Psychology* 68:3-12.

Pollner, Melvin. 1974. "Mundane Reasoning," *Philosophy of the Social Sciences* 4:35-54.

———. 1975. "The Very Coinage of Your Brain," *Philosophy of the Social Sciences* 5:411-430.

Psathas, George, ed. 1979. *Everyday Language*. New York: Wiley.

Pynchon, Thomas. 1973. *Gravity's Rainbow*. New York: Viking.

Rock, P. E. 1968. "Review of Aaron Cicourel, *The Social Organization of Juvenile Justice*," *British Journal of Sociology* 19:474-475.

Rosenfeld, Howard, and Donald Baer. 1969. "Unnoticed Verbal Conditioning of an Aware Experimenter by a More Aware Subject: The Double Agent Effect," *Psychological Review* 76:425-432.

Rossner, Judith. 1977. *Attachments*. New York: Pocket Books.

Roy, Donald. 1952. "Quota Restriction and Goldbricking in a Machine Shop," *American Journal of Sociology* 57:427-442.

———. 1954. "Efficiency and 'The Fix': Informal Intergroup Relations in a Piecework Machine Shop," *American Journal of Sociology* 60:255-266.

Sacks, Harvey, and Emanuel Schegloff. 1979. "Two Preferences in the Organization of Reference to Persons in Conversation and Their Interactions," in *Everyday Language*, pp. 15-22, ed. George Psathas. New York: Wiley.

———, Emanuel Schegloff, and Gail Jefferson. 1978. "A Simplest Systematics for the Organization of Turn Taking for Conversation," in *Studies in the Organization of Conversational Interaction*, pp. 7-56, ed. Jim Schenkein. New York: Academic Press.

Sanders, William. 1977. *Detective Work*. New York: Free Press.

Scheff, Thomas. 1975. "Negotiating Reality: Notes on Power in the Assignment of Responsibility," in *Life as Theater*, pp. 205-218, ed. Dennis Brissett and Charles Edgley. Chicago: Aldine.

Schegloff, Emmanuel. 1968. "Sequencing in Conversational Openings," *American Anthropologist* 70:1075-1095.

———. 1979. "Identification and Recognition in Telephone Conversation Openings," in *Everyday Language*, pp. 23-78, ed. George Psathas. New York: Wiley.

———, and Harvey Sacks. 1974. "Opening Up Closings," in *Ethnomethodology*, pp. 233-264, ed. Roy Turner. Baltimore: Penguin.

Schelling, Thomas. 1960. *The Strategy of Conflict*. New York: Oxford University Press.

———. 1979. *Micromotives and Macrobehavior*. New York: Norton.

Schenkein, Jim, ed. 1978. *Studies in the Organization of Conversational Interaction*. New York: Academic Press.

Schutz, Alfred. 1964. *Collected Papers II. Studies in Social Theory*. The Hague: Martinus Nijhoff.

———. 1967. *Collected Papers I. The Problem of Social Reality*. The Hague: Martinus Nijhoff.

Shibutani, Tamotsu. 1973. "On the Personification of Adversaries," in *Human Nature and Collective Behavior,* pp. 223-233. New Brunswick, N.J.: Transaction.

Spealman, Roger. 1979. "Behavior Maintained by Termination of a Schedule of Self-administered Cocaine," *Science* 204:1231-1233.

Stoddart, Kenneth. 1974. "The Facts of Life About Dope," *Urban Life and Culture* 3:179-204.

Sudnow, David, ed. 1972. *Studies in Social Interaction.* New York: Free Press.

Swanson, Guy, Anthony Wallace, and James Coleman. 1968. "Review Symposium of Harold Garfinkel, *Studies in Ethnomethodology,*" *American Sociological Review* 33:122-130.

Tiryakian, Edward. 1974. "Review of *Studies in Social Interaction* edited by David Sudnow," *Social Forces* 52:567-569.

Toch, Hans, and Richard Schulte. 1968. "Readiness to Perceive Violence as a Result of Police Training," in *Social Perception,* pp. 152-158, ed. Hans Toch and Henry Smith. New York: Van Nostrand.

Touhey, John. 1973. *"Review of Studies in Social Interaction,* edited by David Sudnow," *Contemporary Sociology* 2:504-506.

Toulmin, Stephen. 1961. *Foresight and Understanding.* New York: Harper & Row, Pub.

Turner, Roy, ed. 1974. *Ethnomethodology.* Baltimore: Penguin.

Wagner, Helmut. 1974. "Types of Sociological Theory," in *Theories and Paradigms in Contemporary Sociology,* pp. 41-52, eds R. Serge Denisoff, Orel Callahan, and Mark Levine. Itasca, Ill.: Peacock.

Warriner, Charles. 1973. "The Nature and Functions of Official Morality," in *What We Say/What We Do,* pp. 50-55, ed. Irwin Deutscher. Glenview, Ill.: Scott, Foresman.

Watson, James. 1969. *The Double Helix.* New York: Signet.

Wedow, Suzanne. 1979. "Feeling Paranoid: The Organization of an Ideology About Drug Abuse," *Urban Life* 8:72-93.

West, Candace. 1979. "Against Our Will: Male Interruptions of Females in Cross-Sex Conversation," *Annals of the New York Academy of Science: Language, Sex, and Gender* 327:81-96.

———, **and Don Zimmerman.** 1977. "Women's Place in Everyday Talk: Reflections on Parent-Child Interaction," *Social Problems* 24:521-529.

Wieder, D. L. 1974. "Telling the Code," in *Ethnomethodology,* pp. 144-172, ed. Roy Turner. Baltimore: Penguin.

———, **and Don Zimmerman.** 1974. "Generational Experience and the Development of Freak Culture," *Journal of Social Issues* 30:137-161.

———, **and Don Zimmerman.** 1976. "Becoming a Freak," *Youth and Society* 7:311-344.

Wilkins, James. 1968. "Review of Harold Garfinkel, *Studies in Ethnomethodology,*" *American Journal of Sociology* 73:642-643.

Williams, Michael. 1977. *Groundless Belief.* New Haven, Conn.: Yale University Press.

Wilson, Thomas. 1970. "Conceptions of Interaction and Forms of Sociological Explanation," *American Sociological Review* 35:697-710.

Winch, Peter. 1958. *The Idea of a Social Science.* New York: Humanities Press.

Wittreich, Warren. 1968. "The Honi Phenomenon: A Case Study of Selective Perceptual Distortion," in *Social Perception*, pp. 73-83, ed. Hans Toch and Henry Smith. New York: Van Nostrand.

Wuebben, Paul, Bruce Straits, and Gary Schulman, eds. 1974. *The Experiment as a Social Occasion.* Berkeley, Calif.: Glendessary Press.

Ziman, John. 1978. *Reliable Knowledge: An Exploration of the Grounds for Belief in Science.* Cambridge: Cambridge University Press.

Zimmerman, Don. 1970. "The Practicalities of Rule Use," in *Understanding Everyday Life*, pp. 221-238, ed. J. Douglas. Chicago: Aldine.

———, and P. Lawrence Wieder. 1970. "Ethnomethodology and the Problem of Order: Comment on Denzin," in *Understanding Everyday Life*, pp. 287-298, ed. Jack Douglas. Chicago: Aldine.

Author
Index

Subject
Index